Edited & written by Barclay Price

with contributions
and assistance from
Ian Dobbie, Tony Ford,
Amanda Hare, David Kay,
Morris Latham, Frances
Lord, Sydney Levinson,
Liz Lydiate and Wendy Shales

Running a Workshop
Basic Business for Craftspeople

Crafts Council 1985
Revised edition 1997

ISBN 1 870145 73 9

Published by the Crafts Council
44a Pentonville Road
Islington London N1 9BY

Designed by Pentagram
Printed in Great Britain by
The Ipswich Book Company

Front Cover: Bob Crooks in his
glass studio in London
Photograph by Geoff Waring

Contents

Foreword

Recent research by the Crafts Council shows that craftsmen and women have earnings below the national average and that their major worries are business problems, especially selling. In response the Crafts Council produced 'Running A Workshop', of which this is the latest revised edition, and to date the book has sold over 8,000 copies. No book can hope to be a complete guide to setting up and running a workshop, but we have tried to cover the problems in enough detail to warn the reader of pitfalls and show where to go for further advice.

We realise that craftspeople do not wish to become multi-national corporations but most are interested in seeing their work sold and in a fair return for their efforts. What this book aims to do, therefore, is to give straightforward advice and information relevant to the small size of most craft businesses. As a result, we hope those businesses will run more effectively, and make more profit.

Of the craftspeople supported by the Crafts Council 80% are still successfully running their craft businesses after ten years, a remarkably high percentage for small businesses and an indication that the market for contemporary crafts continues to grow. The sales of crafts within this country and abroad are beginning to form a significant slice of the economy. We hope that this book will encourage others to join in this success story.

Further information on crafts and craft businesses in England and Wales is obtainable from the Crafts Council.

Tony Ford
Director, Crafts Council, 1997

Planning

Whatever your reasons for wanting to set up as a maker, it is important to be realistic. While a career in crafts can be stimulating and creatively rewarding, it also is likely to entail working long hours for a limited financial return. Like anyone running a small business you will need to be determined if you are to survive the normally difficult initial years.

Before going any further, you must sit down and look at the potential for your work. It could be useful to spend time in an established workshop where you will gain valuable insights into the realities of working in crafts. At the very least, talk to a number of craftsmen and women about their experiences. It is also useful to talk over your plans with friends and relations whose views you trust and respect, before committing yourself.

Obtaining advice

Running a crafts business involves a range of skills over and above making work and it is certain that there will be some aspects of running a business with which you are less skilled. Hopefully this book, and the other publications referred to, will assist to some extent but it may be useful for you to obtain training in specific aspects of running the business.

There are many agencies now offering training in starting in business and it is worth investigating what is on offer. The more specific the training is to your craft, or at least to one or two person scale businesses, the more likely it is to be of help to you. Some Regional Arts Boards offer specific training for craftspeople and even if they cannot help directly it is worth contacting your Board as they may be able to offer advice on suitable schemes. A list of these is contained in the final chapter.

Research

If you are to succeed it is essential that you carry out preliminary research before going ahead. Time spent on initial research and planning will save money and effort in the long run.

Research shows that those starting businesses who obtain advice, undertake business training and gather relevant information have a far higher chance of survival than those who do not; thus it is important to prepare yourself and take advice. Such advice can help you solve or circumvent problems, calculate risks and take appropriate action to deal with unexpected incidents.

Market research

You should carry out market research to see if there is likely to be a market for the work you plan to make. That a few of the objects you have made have been admired or bought by friends does not necessarily mean that you can run a successful business. It is wise to try and get a wider response to your work before committing yourself to the expense of setting up in business. Visit craft galleries and shops, craft fairs, look at work in magazines, etc. to get an idea of the likely context and price for your work.

Workspace and equipment

You will need to investigate workshop space and equipment and this is explored in the relevant chapter. Without this preparatory research, it will be difficult to assess the finance you will need.

Finance

To start up in business requires money (capital) to rent premises, buy equipment and materials, promote your work and see you through the initial months before cash from sales starts to come in.

The critical period for most businesses is in the first two to three years and it is during this initial phase that most business failures take place. The reason for this is normally lack of cash. Thus you must ensure that you have enough money to support yourself through this period. The next chapter offers advice on grants and banks. Many craftspeople supplement their business income by other work and it may be sensible to start the business on a part-time basis until you see the level of demand for your work increase.

Setting Objectives

Given the ups and downs experienced by everyone setting up in business on their own and the demands of running a crafts business it is all too easy to get side-tracked and lose direction or to find that commitments entered into turn out not to be the best ones.

Therefore being clear and realistic about your objectives is important; having a lot of exhibitions would not be a good decision if you sold nothing and were forced out of business. Everyone's objectives will be different; one craftsperson may plan to have an annual turnover of £15,000 after two years, own a house with a workshop in the country and sell through ten outlets, while another hopes to achieve a £30,000 turnover, work mainly to commission and be featured in a national magazine. Different objectives will necessitate different approaches.

Setting down a list of objectives does not necessarily mean having a rigid plan. Unforeseen opportunities may arise which, although taking you in a completely different direction from that planned seem absolutely right. However a decision on whether to change direction may be easier to take by previously having thought about what you wish to achieve.

And while your objectives should be realistic they need not be restricted only to what seems possible at that moment. Including objectives that may seem hard to achieve can be useful for there may be ways you can work towards realising your ambitions.

A common problem for craftspeople is pressure on their time and yet many admit that they find it difficult to say no to the many requests which they receive. Being asked to do anything is flattering but unless you are clear as to why you are accepting that particular invitation you may find that the commitment hinders you from taking up a later, more appropriate request. Learning to say no is important if you are to feel in control of your direction.

List of objectives

It helps to write down a list of your objectives divided into specific periods. In this example objectives are set for the next six months, year, two years and five years :

In 6 months :
– have purchased all necessary equipment
– have work in six different galleries
– obtain coverage in three relevant magazines
– print a promotional postcard

In 1 year :
– participate in a group exhibition in London
– have work in a further four galleries

In 2 years :
– attend Chelsea Crafts Fair
– be selling in a number of countries abroad
– have a part-time teaching job at a London college
– have a one person exhibition

 In 5 years :
– have a workshop/home out of London
– have a turnover of £50,000

Spend time preparing your list. It can be helpful to discuss it with someone who knows you and your work and whose views you value. Talking it over with someone will help clarify your thoughts.

If we take the example above, were this maker to be approached soon after preparing their list of objectives by a gallery in Wales offering them a one person exhibition they might decide that as this would preclude spending the next few months finding the ten outlets and supplying work to these, they would be best to say no. On the other hand they might decide that the gallery offer was appropriate as it was a good gallery, agree to the exhibition and revise their objectives accordingly.

Similarly an approach from a Guild to undertake a weekend demonstration might be turned down by the maker as this would not help achieve their aims. However a short-term residency in a college might be accepted as it would provide experience and contacts which could assist in achieving the aim of a part-time teaching post in the future.

Having such a list will enable you periodically to match reality against your original objectives and assess your relative success or failure without allowing your judgement to be coloured too much by either depression or temporary euphoria.

Your list of objectives need not only be used as a check list against requests from others. It can also assist you in targeting your time and tasks and drawing up an Action Plan can assist with time management.

Action Plan

An action plan can help define the tasks you need to undertake to work towards your objectives and establish target dates by which you intend to achieve these. This can help focus your time and stop you from being distracted from essential tasks. Again it can be helpful to talk through your Action Plan with a friend as explaining why you plan to do X to achieve Y will help clarify your thinking and your friend may well suggest alternative ways that you had not considered.

Thus, based on the example objectives, the Action Plan over the next six month period might be:

Within the next fortnight :

- Prepare detailed list and prices of essential equipment
- Research possible galleries to approach

Within one month :

- Have ordered the main items of equipment
- Contact at least six galleries

Within two months

- Contact further six galleries
- Research possible magazines to approach for coverage
- Have some photographs of recent work taken

Within three months

- Select ten magazines, find out whom to approach and write
- Contact further six galleries, if required

Within six months

- Contact possible London spaces where you could participate in a group exhibition

14 Revise your objectives as your career develops and update your Action Plan on a regular basis.

Business Plan

A Business Plan is a useful tool in presenting your work and business idea to other agencies and essential if you are approaching a bank or other institution to borrow money or applying for a grant.

Most funding agencies expect applicants to present Business Plans and presenting a professional Business Plan may be a factor in successfully obtaining assistance.

A Business Plan should contain the following :

– description of the business
– market research undertaken
– type of work to be produced
– pricing of the work
– plan of action
– what finance is required for
– level of finance required
– cash flow
– curriculum vitae

plus any relevant photographs, press cuttings, etc.

INTRODUCTION

I plan to set up a small workshop making one off studio ceramics.

The success of my degree show has led to a number of offers for exhibitions during the next two years and I will be producing work for these. In addition
I shall be producing a range of decorated tableware which I plan to sell through upmarket department stores, both in this country and abroad.

MARKET RESEARCH

The following galleries have expressed interest in exhibiting my work:
The Cambridge Gallery, Cambridge, Craft Scene, Ipswich,
New Designs, London, New Ceramics, London, New Directions, Glasgow and Ceramique, Paris. As a result of a college project I became involved with Right Plates Ltd who have commissioned me to undertake a series of designs for tableware. They will be marketing these and paying me a royalty.

PRICING

I have costed my work and looked at how the cost price relates to similar work on sale in galleries. The selling prices of my ceramics will be between £140 and £230 (presuming 100% mark up plus VAT) and I have discussed this with gallery owners who feel confident that the work can sell at this price. I will be receiving a royalty advance of £250 from Bright Plates Ltd.

PREMISES

I have already found a workshop space and am negotiating a renewable lease. It is owned by London Enterprise Workshops Ltd and initially will be let to me on a two year lease. The cost is £300 per month (to include all charges except electricity) for the first two years rising to £400 in the third year. The workshop, in Hackney, London, is 440 sq. feet. It has water but will require three phase electricity. This has been costed.
I estimate that the timetable for commencing production is :

MAY:
- Sign workshop lease, order kiln & phone
- Arrange for three phase to be connected

JUNE :
- Redecorate & build shelving, etc.
- Buy other items of equipment and install

JULY:
- Install kiln. Carry out test firings. Produce design work for Bright Plates Ltd
- Commence full scale production

WORKSHOP CAPITAL COSTS	
Three phase electricity	£ 480
Ventilation & extraction	£ 450
Painting, shelving, etc.	£ 230
Install telephone	£ 70
Total	£ 1,230

EQUIPMENT REQUIRED

I already own a test kiln, spray gun & booth and various hand tools.
I need to purchase :

Laser Kiln (Electric) 12 cubic feet Model HGF675 (includes full controls)	£ 3,200 (inc vat)
Wheel	£ 245 (inc vat)
Ratcliffes Mixers & tub	£ 120 (inc vat)
Total	£ 3,565

FINANCE REQUIRED

The enclosed Cash Flow includes the initial set up costs, purchase of equipment and all the costs of running the business. Income from sales is based on average monthly sales plus additional sales at major Craft Fair in October and Christmas orders. For most of these sales I have estimated receiving payment within six weeks. I have been awarded a TEC grant and this will start from 1st August. This is £40.00 per week for one year. I have also been awarded a Crafts Council equipment grant which will be about £1,800 (50% of the cost of equipment).

I have an agreed advance against royalty payments from Bright Plates and a teaching block in February and this income is included.

I shall be investing £2,000 which I have saved.

I am applying for a loan of £2,000 and a flexible overdraft facility with an upper limit of £3,500 although as my Cash Flow indicates I would hope to reduce this in Year Two. I have made allowance of £150 per month for bank interest and loan repayments.

18 CURRICULUM VITAE

1968	Born in Liverpool
1988	Arts Foundation Course, Bristol Poly
1989-92	Ceramics Degree (BA 2.1)
	University of West England
1993	LEntA Design Enterprise Training (8 weeks)

EXHIBITIONS

1989	Young Clay: Mall Galleries, London
	New Designers, London
1990	Out of Clay: Cambridge Gallery
1992	Bonhams Contemporary Art Auction
	New Spirit: Keramik Studio, Vienna
	University of West England
1993	New Ceramics, London

EXHIBITIONS ARRANGED

1994	Creative Ceramics: Festival Hall, London
	New Directions, Glasgow
	Ceramique, Paris
	A New Decade : British Council touring exhibition to Japan

AWARDS

New Tableware Award 1989: British Tableware Federation

Crafts Council Setting Up Grant

ACCOMPANYING INFORMATION

Photographs of recent work

Article on my work from "Interiors" magazine July 1993.

Cash Flow

A Cash Flow is a key part of a Business Plan and even if you decide not to prepare a Business Plan you should draw up a Cash Flow forecast for the first year of the business.

A Cash Flow is a method of forecasting how much money will come into the business and how much will be spent. It is quite simply an estimate of how much you think you will earn and how much you think you will spend over a future period. As it can only be an estimate you must work out as best you can what money you think will come in and be paid out. For the basis of the forecast all income, whether cheques or cash, is counted.

One of the main reasons for new businesses failing is that they run out of cash during the first year or two and anything you can do to predict your business's needs over a longer period and so plan within the finance available will make it more likely that your business will survive.

When starting a new business there can be a tendency to look only at the cash required to get it up and running and not recognise the need for cash to keep things going until income from sales starts to come in. Even where orders have been secured before starting, perhaps from a college show, it will be some time before payment is received for these sales.

If you are approaching a bank or other institution for a loan or overdraft then the Cash Flow enables them to see the level of funding required and how this will be repaid over a future period. For yourself, the Cash Flow may show that you need to borrow more money than you originally anticipated or find a part-time job to help pay your bills.

 Cash Flow projections are normally prepared for one year and tabled month by month as detailed in the example. (The example is for a ten month period for reasons of space).

The monthly projections which you make should then be checked regularly against the actual monthly figures so that you can see whether the actual position is worse or better.

In estimating income you must remember that invoices for sales will not normally be paid for a time, so when you are estimating the income from any sales billed by invoice you should presume that at least two months will elapse before the actual cash is received. For a cash flow statement it is advisable to be pessimistic rather than optimistic.

While a Cash Flow is particularly critical at the launch of a new business and essential at any time when approaching a bank or other institution for financial support, it is also a useful tool for all businesses to continue to use to keep them aware of future financial needs. A Cash Flow can be particularly useful in situations where there will be an unusually high expenditure prior to the money from sales coming in – such as where you are working on a major commission or attending an important craft or trade fair. To use the last as an example, there will be bills to pay in advance including the fee for the event, production of publicity material, travel, etc. and the cost of making a stock of work. However no cash will come in until the event or later and a Cash Flow will show whether there is sufficient money to work towards the event or a need to borrow money to fund the activity.

	Notes	Jun	Jul	Aug
INCOME				
Sale of work	1	–	400	400
Design fees (Brights)	1	–	250	–
Teaching	2	–	–	–
Savings	3	2000	–	–
TEC grant	4	215	215	215
Crafts Council grant	4	–	1800	–
Loan requested	5	2000	–	–
Total estimated income	**-**	**4215**	**2665**	**615**
EXPENDITURE				
1. Start up costs	6	–	–	–
Equipment purchases	–	3565	–	–
Workshop capital costs	–	1230	–	–
2. Running costs	7			
Rent/Rates	–	300	300	300
Electricity/Gas		–	200	–
Motor expenses	–	120	120	120
Telephone/postage	–	50	30	135
Craft Fair Fees	–	–	430	–
Craft Fair costs		–	–	–
Photography	–	–	350	–
Postcards	–	–	–	–
Accountant/insurance	–	340	–	–
Sundries	–	50	50	50
Repairs/cleaning		40	40	40
Materials	8	200	–	–
Sub-total	–	**5895**	**1520**	**645**
Cash drawings	9	250	250	250
Loan repayments (est.)	10	150	150	150
Total estimated expenditure		**6295**	**1920**	**1045**
Net loss/profit per month	11	**-2080**	**745**	**-430**
Cumulative loss/profit	12	**-2080**	**-1335**	**-1765**
To be covered by requested overdraft facility of £3,500	13			

Sep	Oct	Nov	Dec	Jan	Feb	Mar
400	2200	2800	1800	3000	800	800
–	–	–	–	–	–	–
–	–	–	–	–	–	800
–	–	–	–	–	–	–
215	215	215	215	215	215	215
–	–	–	–	–	–	–
–	–	–	–	–	–	–
615	**2415**	**3015**	**2015**	**3215**	**1015**	**1815**
–	–	–	–	–	–	–
–	–	–	–	–	–	–
–	–	–	–	–	–	–
300	300	300	300	300	300	300
–	390	–	–	320	–	–
120	380	120	250	120	120	120
50	50	190	50	50	230	50
350	–	–	–	–	–	400
–	500	–	250	–	–	–
–	–	–	–	–	450	–
200	–	–	–	–	–	200
–	–	–	–	–	350	–
50	50	50	50	50	50	50
40	40	40	40	40	40	40
300	500	200	200	300	200	200
1410	**2210**	**900**	**1140**	**1180**	**1740**	**1360**
250	250	250	250	250	250	250
150	150	150	150	150	150	150
1810	**2610**	**1300**	**1540**	**1580**	**2140**	**1760**
-1195	**-195**	**1715**	**475**	**1635**	**-1125**	**55**
-2960	**-3155**	**-1440**	**-965**	**670**	**-455**	**-400**

NOTES TO CASH FLOW

1) All the income you estimate to receive each month from sales of work or designs. As this is a cash flow put amounts under the month you expect to receive payment – e.g. work sold to a gallery in June may not be paid for until August.

2) You may decide to keep income from other work, such as teaching, separate. However if applying for a loan it may be useful to include such income in the Cash Flow to show your ability to repay the loan.

3) If you are using savings or funds from elsewhere (your own savings or a loan from a relative for example) then show this as being introduced into the business.

4) Include grants received towards the business and as this is a provisional document you may decide to include grants you are applying for with some realistic expectation of success. However if you are unsuccessful you would need to adjust things accordingly and given that in such a case your borrowing requirement would increase you might be best to leave anything unconfirmed out and if successful you can then please the bank manager by asking for less!

5) Include the loan you are applying for.

6) It can be useful, particularly where the business is just starting, to show the initial installation and equipment costs as separate items.

7) These are the general running costs of the business. They do not include personal expenditure such as rent of your flat.

8) The cost of materials you expect to have to buy. Remember that as sales increase so will expenditure on materials.

9) Cash drawings is the term for the money which self-employed people take out of the business in lieu of wages. Unless you are going to live off other income (another job for example) you should include a regular amount to cover your personal bills.

10) You are unlikely to know what the repayments will be. However put an estimate in this column and adjust it once you have spoken to the bank or whoever you are applying to for the loan. If it is more then remember your borrowing requirement will rise.

11) This is the net position each month. Thus in July you have estimated £2,665 of income and £1,920 of expenditure thus the net monthly result is a profit of £745 whereas in August there is net loss of £430.

12) This is the important section of the Cash Flow for this shows the cumulative result by combining each month's results. If your bank account started at zero then this would be the estimated balance at the end of each month. It estimates your maximum borrowing requirement (after taking into account the loan) to be £3,155 (in October) and shows that in January you move into credit but return to the 'red' in February.

13) Given that the Cash Flow shows the maximum need (after taking into account the £2,000 loan) to be for an overdraft of £3,155 James Potter has requested a limit of £3,500 so that he has some flexibility should things be a little different from these estimates.

Financing the Business

 All new businesses need to invest money at the beginning. With a crafts business money is required to buy equipment, fit out/set up a workspace and sustain the period of production before sales begin to bring cash into the business.

Research indicates that one of the commonest reasons for new businesses failing is under-estimating the cash required and so running into cash flow difficulties. Therefore it is essential to ensure that you have sufficient money to cover the start up costs and see you through the initial period before your business begins to break even or move into profit.

There are four main ways in which new craft businesses tend to be financed. Personal savings, a loan from a friend or relation, a grant or a loan/overdraft from a bank or other financial institution.

Even if you have been running your workshop for a time and have an income from sales, it is likely that at some point you will require extra funds to buy bulk materials for stock, replace or buy new equipment, finance a large commission or build up work for an exhibition or craft fair. Unless you are fortunate enough to have sufficient resources of your own, you will need to obtain funding from elsewhere, which means applying for a grant or loan.

Making a grant application
The final chapter gives information on possible sources of grants. Obtain information on all that could be relevant and carefully check the information to see if you are eligible to apply for that particular scheme. If so, apply! While not everyone who applies will be successful it is certain that those who do not try will have no chance at all.

Grant-giving bodies often ask you to complete an application form. This is likely to be their first contact with you so it helps if you try to make a good impression. Take care to check the information to ensure that you are eligible and that you provide all the information requested. If possible, type your entries; it looks more professional and is easier to read than handwriting. If you cannot type, always use black ink as it photocopies clearly and write legibly. This may seem petty, but when a committee has a hundred or more applications to go through it makes life much easier. If there is no application form, using headed notepaper looks more professional.

Always do a trial run on paper, or better still on a photocopy of the form; it saves making mistakes, and you can keep the copy for reference. Before returning the application, check that you have enclosed the supporting material asked for. There is usually a good reason why 35mm slides rather than photographs are wanted, for instance, and failure to send the correct visual evidence of work can cause delay in processing the application or make the application ineligible.

When you submit slides, photographs, illustrations or any loose sheets of information, label each one with your name; for slides, use self-adhesive labels because the ones you lick with your tongue tend to detach themselves and jam the slide projector. Indicate which way up each slide should be shown and pack them carefully in a plastic slide wallet, if you send them loose in an ordinary envelope they are likely to be damaged in the post. Always send a list describing your slides or photographs (materials used, size, date made, etc.). In most cases this will be asked for on the application form.

Good visual evidence of your work is essential. First-stage decisions are often made on the basis of slides or photographs, so weak pictures are as bad as no pictures. The photograpy chapter provides detailed information on preparation and presentation of photographs.

What else should accompany your application? A folder with any press clippings or other information may be useful. Your curriculum vitae should be up to date and, apart from giving your name, address and training, it should list grants, awards, exhibitions, major commissions and publications in which you have appeared. It should also mention any relevant work experience you have had. A short, unpretentious statement about your work will interest people, especially if it includes details about materials and any special methods used. Send only what is relevant. Committee members will not welcome having to wade through masses of paper that has no direct bearing on the application. You will find that most organisations are unable to accept actual pieces of work at the first stages of selection because of the administrative problems involved.

Try and find out as much as you can about the organisation you are applying to and what they will be looking for. The Crafts Council, for instance, has copies of slides of Setting-Up Grant recipients' work which can be viewed at in the Information Section during opening hours. It may be useful to know who will be on the committee and most organisations will be happy to tell you this. Do not be afraid to ask any questions you may have about the particular scheme you are applying under, but check these are not already answered in the accompanying guidelines! If you have several queries, it may be worth telephoning the person responsible for administering the scheme before actually completing the form.

Make sure that the application and accompanying information arrive a few days before the deadline. Finally, try not to be too despondent if your application is rejected. Most selection processes are very competitive, with only a small number of applicants being successful.

Banks

It is likely that at some point you will look to your bank to lend you some money. It is equally likely that you already have an overdraft and maybe also the ccompanying letters of regret from your bank manager! The first point to make is that if your relationship with your bank is a bad one, then it is perhaps best to close that account and move to another bank. This can be particularly relevant if you are just leaving college, as inadequate student grants may have led to a stormy relationship. If you open an account with another bank you will have a fresh start.

Banks will tend to charge substantially for business accounts. Some banks offer free banking for a first year to small businesses and this is worth investigating. However if the level of turnover in the first few years is likely to be limited then it may be worth opening an account in a building society to use as your business account as these are normally free of charges.

Whether you are starting your workshop business or developing it, you should try to borrow enough money to help you function through the first difficult months. You may decide to operate by having an overdraft and/or loan, but in either case you must arrange this with your bank manager in advance. There is no point in trying to operate on an overdraft only to have your cheques suddenly bounce because you did not get permission to increase your overdraft limit. If this happens, your business will be in trouble as suppliers will not accept your cheques or give you credit.

An overdraft is the most common form of funding for a small business, the advantage being that interest is calculated on the actual level of borrowing day to day (usually 2-3% over bank base rate). The disadvantage is that it is less secure than a loan and the interest rate will fluctuate in line with the bank rate.

 A bank loan is normally only given for a specific purpose, such as buying equipment or renovating your workshop. The advantage of a loan is that you receive a specific sum of money and know in advance the regular repayments which must be made. Loans are normally given for one to five years and cost slightly more than an overdraft. It is quite possible to borrow in both ways; a loan for equipment and an overdraft for day-to-day running costs.

Approaching a bank manager can be unnerving, but remember that a bank's business is lending money so you should not feel embarrassed about asking. Try and present yourself in a professional way. You should prepare a Business Plan (see previous chapter).

Prepare your Business Plan in advance and send it to your bank manager with a letter requesting an appointment. If you have photos of your work or newspaper cuttings, include copies as anything that emphasises your serious approach can only help. When you go along for the appointment, make sure that you know exactly how much of a loan or overdraft you require and what security you could offer, if any.

The simplest form of bank security is to have the loan guaranteed by someone whom the bank trusts to repay the loan, should you not. This can be a more business-like way of obtaining help from a relative or friend; you might be doubtful about asking them for cash straight out, but asking them to act a guarantor may be more acceptable. Also they will not actually have to put up any cash – unless your business fails. Other types of security include property, other funds such as a building society account, stocks and shares, etc. It can be useful to take along one or more pieces of work so that the manager can see what you make and the quality of the making.

Even if you have no security it may still be possible to get some help if the bank thinks your ideas are well thought through and your approach professional.

If you are successful in obtaining a loan or overdraft, ensure that you keep the bank informed. If you start running into financial difficulties, tell the bank in advance rather than waiting for them to find out. If you receive any publicity or have an exhibition, let your bank manager know.

If you are unsuccessful in obtaining assistance from one bank it may be worth trying another.

There are a series of schemes designed to assist small businesses with borrowing, although these tend to be less relevant to very small businesses. However, it may be worth asking your bank about the government-backed Loan Guarantee Scheme or any similar scheme operated by the bank itself.

Administration

Administration

All too often self-employed businesses fail not because of their work but as a result of inadequate administration. This chapter is designed to help you tackle the basic administrative tasks involved in running your business.

The first essential is to sort out your tax and national insurance (NI) position. If you are running your own business, you are technically ineligible for Unemployment Benefit or Supplementary Benefit. However, certain local offices do allow some flexibility to people starting up in business; explain that you are about to set up but will have no income for the initial period, and ask their advice about continuing to draw benefit. If you clarify your tax and Nl position as soon as possible after you set up, you will avoid difficulties later.

It is common for craftspeople to combine employment and self-employment. The fact that you may be employed elsewhere for part of the time does not preclude you from becoming self-employed or vice versa. If you are earning money from your self-employment, even if you have a part- or full-time job, then you are required to fulfil the tax and national insurance requirements that relate to self-employed people.

Again, if you organise book-keeping and paperwork systems early on you will make life easier; the longer you leave these jobs, the more complicated they become. People often shy away from book-keeping and other necessary paperwork because they seem complex, but it is perfectly possible to set up simple systems which work well for most craft businesses.

Administration cannot be avoided so the most realistic approach is to come to terms with it. You may never reach the stage where you enjoy book-keeping and other administrative tasks, but at least you can reduce the amount of worry and time expended on them by understanding what needs to be done, organising a system that suits you, and dealing with it on a regular basis.

It can be advantageous to contact an accountant before starting your business or at an early stage as there are points such as the start date of businesses, capital purchases and transfers of personal capital assets to the business where an accountant's advice may be beneficial from a tax situation. Also an accountant can offer advice on a suitable way of keeping your books which will entail them in less work at the year end and so reduce their bill.

The legal framework of the business

Almost every craftsman or woman starts their business by "working for themselves", i.e. technically they become SOLE TRADERS. A few team up with one or more like-minded individuals and without further formalities start work; they are PARTNERS. And there are a very few who from the beginning set up a LIMITED COMPANY or a CO-OPERATIVE.

SOLE TRADER

This is the simplest form of business set-up requiring no legal formalities whatsoever, only a private decision to start trading.

For most new crafts businesses it is the obvious choice; the craftsperson is in complete control and takes all the profit (or loss!), there are no legal setting up costs and minimal paperwork. The tax position may also be slightly advantageous in the case of a young business. There is nothing to stop a sole trader from taking on employees.

The main disadvantage of this form of trading is that if the business fails, creditors can take legal action not only against business assets for the money owed to them, but also against any private assets, for example your house. This is why businessmen and women sometimes transfer major assets into their spouse's name so that these will not be at risk. (They are, of course, running another risk in the event of a divorce.)

Although this form of business requires no legal formalities to commence, both the DSS and the Inland Revenue must be informed and you will be required to pay National Insurance (unless exempt) and income tax on the profits of the business.

If you decide to trade under any name other than your own (for example, as " Blackbird Pottery" rather than Anthony Potter or A. Potter), whilst you no longer have to register a business name, you must disclose the real name and address of the owner on all business paperwork including letters, orders, invoices and receipts. In addition you must display this information clearly in any business premises to which customers and suppliers have access. Full details of the requirements are available from Training Enterprise Councils.

PARTNERSHIP

A partnership is merely an extension of the set-up under the previous heading of "sole trader", but in this case two or more people carry on the business and share profits (or losses) between them, usually in equal portions.

No legal formalities are required to set up a partnership and nothing need be stated in writing, but in practice it is of the utmost importance that a written partnership agreement is drawn up, preferably by a solicitor. Partnerships often last a long time and, as in marriages, over the years situations and attitudes change so that when the end comes bitter legal fights can develop over the property acquired.

Have a partnership agreement prepared and signed, and then file it away. You may never need to refer to it but it is there should any arguments arise.

The partnership agreement should cover the following points, as well as any other points relevant to your situation:

- the purpose of the partnership
- the amount of capital to be put in by each partner
- the role of each partner
- the apportionment of profits and losses (e.g. 50/50)
- the arrangements for dissolving the partnership, including the retirement or death of a partner
- how the bank account is to be operated
- the hours of work and holidays allotted
- provision in the event of a long sickness of one partner
- arrangements for arbitration in the event of disagreement.

It is worth taking professional advice when drawing up a partnership agreement.

The advantage of a partnership is that two or more people working together are more cost-effective and bring to the business a range of complementary skills. It can provide moral support; difficult decisions may be easier to take after joint discussions. Like the sole trader, a business run as a partnership is cheap to set up, with no legal formalities, and it can employ others. The requirements to inform the DSS and the Inland Revenue and-to disclose the names of the proprietors are exactly the same.

In a partnership it is important to note that each partner is responsible for the business debts and errors of the other(s). Thus, if the business fails and one partner does not pay their share of the debts, the other partner(s) will be required to pay not only their own share but also the share of the first partner. This even extends to tax debts. In a partnership you assume responsibility for all debts incurred by the business even if they were incurred by another partner's dishonesty or mismanagement without your knowledge, so think very carefully before entering into a partnership.

For a small crafts business the advantages of having someone to talk to or of sharing machinery may be gained merely by sharing a workshop. In such a case you do not have to be partners.

LIMITED COMPANY

Some businesses are set up from the start as limited companies, while other sole traders or partnerships may decide to turn themselves into a limited company as the business grows.

Either way, the main advantage is that, because the limited company has its independent legal identity, the sole trader or partners (who become the director(s) of the company) is liable for no more than the nominal value of the share held in the company. In other words, his/her personal possessions are not at risk. Another possible advantage is that suppliers sometimes treat a company, albeit small, with greater respect than they do a sole trader. However, the advantages are not especially great, because a bank manager lending money to a small limited company, or a landlord granting a lease to one, will usually insist that the director gives a personal guarantee. Thus the advantage of the limited liability is largely eroded. Furthermore, it is quite expensive to set up a company, record-keeping is likely to be more extensive and accountants' fees therefore higher.

Clearly, before setting up a limited company it will be worth discussing all the pros and cons with your accountant, bank manager and solicitor.

For those who have substantial turnovers or are involved in large scale, high value projects such as major commissions where there is substantial financial risk were things to go wrong, then setting up a company may be worth considering.

Co-operative

Craftspeople who are intending to work in some joint situation, perhaps by sharing a workshop, are sometimes tempted to think that by setting up a co-operative the problems of joint decision-making will be solved. They will not and craftspeople who, by definition, are producing and selling individual work will almost certainly find that the co-operative structure will not allow them sufficient control over their own businesses.

Further information on co-operatives can be obtained from :

Co-operative Union Ltd
Holyoake House
Hanover Street
Manchester, M60 OAS
0161 832 4300
Organising body for co-operative movement. Organises conferences and training courses. Library and information service available. Produces several publications.

Co-operative Development Agencies
In priority areas, local resource centres give advice and training to help set up co-operatives. Contact Local Enterprise Centre for details on local agencies.

42 **Taxation**

Everyone who receives an income is liable to pay tax on it. Rates of tax are set at a percentage of your taxable income, which is everything you earn or receive from investments less your personal allowance (a fixed amount which varies depending whether you are married or single) and allowances for such things as mortgage interest, dependant relatives, etc. The booklet CWL1 STARTING YOUR OWN BUSINESS published by the Inland Revenue, is extremely helpful in explaining how tax and National Insurance relates to the self-employed. As soon as you start your own business or workshop, you should advise the Department of Social Security using the form CWF1 NOTIFIACTION OF SELF EMPLOYMENT, a copy of which is contained in the booklet CWL1 referred to above. The DSS will then forward the form to your tax office. You should be aware that there are automatic penalities if you fail to register your self employment with the Inland Revenue within six months of the end of the tax year (ending on 5th April) in which your self employment started; for example, if you started on 1 August 1997, which is in the tax year year ending 5 April 1998, you would have to notify the authorities by no later than 5 October 1998. The booklet also conytains a list of other useful leaflets published by the Inland Revenue and DSS.

While it is not impossible for the self-employed to deal directly with their local tax office, most people find it difficult and it is far better to employ an accountant. You are particularly advised to employ an accountant when setting up as the first year is particularly important in relation to tax. He/she will be able to advise on the best date to set for your period of accounting, show you how best to keep your books so as to reduce the work they need to do at the year end, recommend possible transfer of personal capital assets (equipment, car, computer, etc.) to the business and give some idea of your likely tax liability, if any.

An accountant will prepare your annual accounts, taking into consideration all allowable business expenditure, and will negotiate the tax assessment on your behalf with the tax office.

Schedule D Taxation

If you are established as a sole trader or part of a partnership, you are liable for income tax under Schedule D taxation; if you are incorporated as a limited company, you pay Corporation Tax. Under Schedule D tax is payable on your profit, which is the balance of your income left after deducting all expenses incurred wholly and exclusively for the purposes of your business. Your income includes fees and grants, for example a Setting Up or Prince's Youth Business Trust Grant. The main part of your income will come from sales and commissions.

Allowable tax expenses normally include workshop overheads (i.e. rent, rates, light, heat, telephone, travel, postage, motor vehicle expenses, bank charges, interest on loans, bad debts, accountancy and legal fees, materials, etc.). Where certain items, such as your car or telephone, are used for both business and personal purposes, an appropriate proportion of the cost can be claimed. If you are working from home a proportion of the household expenses may also be claimed, but if you own your house be careful about claiming any part of mortgage repayments as any profit from selling the property may be partially assessed for capital gains tax. Check this point with your accountant. Even if you have a workshop away from your home you can claim some allowance for use of the home if you carry out designing or administration there.

Capital expenditures such as the purchase of equipment or a motor vehicle qualify for special allowances; again you should obtain advice from your accountant. If you already own capital equipment that will be used in the business, a motor vehicle, computer, tools, etc., you will be able to take these into the business and treat them as capital purchases by the business although no cash will be involved.

Self Assessment

Since the tax year 1996/97, tax is now accounted for by "Self Assessment", details of which may be found in the Inland Revenue booklet SA/BK2 Self Assessment - a guide for the self employed. Details of your income tax for the tax year must now be supplied to the Inland Revenue by no later than 30 September following the end of the tax year if you want the Inland Revenue to work your tax out for you; otherwise, you must do the calculations yourself, in which case you have until 31 January following the end of the tax year in which to submit the return and pay your tax and Class 4 National Insurance Contributions. If your return is submitted after 31 Janaury, the automatic penalities will apply and tax surcharges and interest may also be applied.

If a loss is made in any one year, this either can be offset against other income (for example, part time work) or carried forward and set against future profits. Also, if you have been employed and paid tax in the preceding three years prior to starting your business you can offset any loss against the tax paid and obtain the relevant tax refund.

You should note, however, that if losses occur regularly over a number of years the Tax Inspector may disallow further claims for relief on the grounds that you are not running a business but merely engageed in a hobby.

Part-time employment when self employed

Many self employed people are also employed by others. Usually this is part-time work, teaching for example, but it is also possible to be employed full-time and still have earnings from self-employment.

It is important to know the difference between being self-employed and employed. When you carry out a commission for someone or work as a sub-contractor you are doing so on a self-employed basis as you are able to choose when and how to carry out the work. However where you are expected to work to someone else's conditions, such as the place or time, you will normally be treated as employed.

Where you are employed your employer will deduct tax from your earnings if you earn over specific amounts.

When you come to the end of your tax year what you have earned from employment (and the tax paid on those earnings) is taken into account with your self-employed earnings to compute your overall tax liability. In the event of you having paid out more tax than you were due then the Inland Revenue will reimburse the overpayment.

If you are likely to make a loss in any year from your self-employment (due to your setting up expenses being greater than your income) and you have part-time employment on which you would normally pay tax, then it can be sensible to request that your Personal Allowance be used against your employment. This has the benefit of saving paying out tax on your part- time earnings which will assist your cash flow.

Choosing an accountant

The best way to find an accountant is to ask for recommendations from friends who are already working in business on their own. If that is not possible, your bank manager may be able to offer advice. Try to find an accountant who is used to dealing with self-employed people, ideally some of whom are craftspeople. Having selected one or more possible people arrange to meet them to see if they are some-one you feel happy dealing with.

Accountants can provide useful advice on book-keeping and it will be helpful to agree your system with your accountant in advance as he/she will be the one who has to understand and organise the information you provide in an appropriate format. Remember that advice may cost money. However sorting a system out in advance that will entail less work for your accountant at the year end is likely to save money in the long term.

Many accountants will be reluctant to quote their likely annual charge, given that they will not know how much advice you require or the state of your books, but it is worth asking for a rough idea. You must remember that the work which will need to be done in the first year when you are setting up, normally will be greater than in subsequent years and therefore the fee for the first year may be higher than in later years. It may be worth shopping around as accountant's fees can vary enormously, although you have to equate the cost with the service each provides. Also it may be worth paying a little more for an accountant you like.

If you feel dissatisfied with the service or the cost, the best thing is to tell the accountant. This may seem obvious but it is all too easy not to say anything, and often talking about a problem can quickly lead to its solution. If you continue to be dissatisfied then you should not hesitate to change to someone else.

National insurance (NI)

If you are self-employed for all or part of the time, you must pay National Insurance contributions unless your profit in a year from self-employment is less than an amount set annually. The 1997/98 figure was £3,480. The leaflet NATIONAL INSURANCE CONTRIBUTIONS FOR SELF-EMPLOYED PEOPLE (CA03) explains what contributions need to be made and SELF-EMPLOYED? (FB30) is a guide to National Insurance and Social Security benefits.

It is important to make sure that you start paying National Insurance contributions or claim exemption when you start in business as failure to do so can lead to prosecution and may involve you in having to pay all the amount in arrears if it is discovered that you have been operating as self-employed but not paying NI contributions.

CLASS 2 CONTRIBUTIONS

These must be paid every week including holidays at the rate of £6.15 (1997/98 rate) unless you have exemption. The best method for paying Class 2 contributions is by arranging for contributions to be automatically paid from your Bank account by direct debit. For further information on paying by direct debit see leaflet CLASS 2 AND CLASS 3 : DIRECT DEBIT, THE EASY WAY TO PAY! (CA04)

EXEMPTION FROM CLASS 2 CONTRIBUTIONS

This can be applied for if your think your profits in the year are going to be less than a certain amount set annually. The 1997/98 figure was £3,480. To apply for exemption obtain the leaflet NI FOR PEOPLE WITH SMALL EARNINGS FROM SELF-EMPLOYMENT (CA02). 'Exemption must be applied for' - you cannot just not pay contributions because your earnings fall below the limit. Do not leave your application too late.

Not paying Class 2 contributions may affect your entitlement to NI benefits although if it is only for a year or two the effect is likely to be negligible. However women who think there is a possibility of their wishing to apply for maternity allowance in the future should take advice as to whether it is in their interests to pay voluntary Class 2 contributions to ensure that they receive maternity allowance.

CLASS 4 CONTRIBUTIONS

These are paid on top of Class 2 contributions and are assessed and collected by the Inland Revenue along with your tax in half-yearly instalments. Class 4 contributions are assessed on the basis of your profits for the year and will be payable if these are more than a certain amount set annually. The 1997/98 figure was 6% of profits exceeding £7,010.

CLASS 1 CONTRIBUTIONS

If you are employed elsewhere for part of the time you will have to pay Class 1 contributions as well if you earn more than a specified amount in any one week or a year.

The 1997/98 figures were more than £62 in a week, more than £268 in a month or more than £3,224 in a year. These contributions will automatically be deducted by your employer. However, there is an upper level to the amount of contributions you have to pay in any one tax year and if your total contributions are more than this the excess will be refunded to you.

In certain circumstances, to avoid the need for a refund you can ask to postpone payment of Class 2 and Class 4 contributions until your exact liability is known - an option worth investigating if you are earning a substantial amount from part-time work.

SOCIAL SECURITY BENEFITS FOR THE SELF-EMPLOYED.

There are a range of possible benefits. Information on these is contained in the leaflet SELF-EMPLOYED? - A GUIDE TO NATIONAL INSURANCE CONTRIBUTIONS AND SOCIAL SECURITY BENEFITS (FB30). This leaflet refers to further information leaflets which provide more detail.

The main areas of possible benefit are :
- Sickness Benefit
- Statutory Sick Pay
- Family Credit
- Maternity Allowance
- Council Tax Benefit
- Housing Benefit

There is a useful booklet " A Guide to Housing Benefit and Council Tax Benefit" RR2 which also may be worth obtaining if you think you may be able to claim. One problem for self-employed people in claiming Housing Benefit is that in certain cases the DSS, unlike the Inland Revenue, may be reluctant to accept your estimate of likely future earnings.

Retirement Pensions

If you have paid sufficient National Insurance payments then you will receive the basic State pension on reaching retirement age. If you have not paid the required full amount over your working life then you will receive the relevant percentage. For information on this obtain the leaflets Retiring? Your pension and other benefits (FB6) and A Guide To Retirement Pensions (NP46).

As the basic state pension is generally considered to be inadequate you may wish to consider investing in additional pension rights, especially as there are substantial tax benefits involved. If so, consult your accountant or an insurance broker for details of the various schemes. Given that earnings from self-employment are likely to fluctuate self-employed people may be better considering a scheme wherein they can vary the payments as this allows for flexibility.

Paperwork

The two main kinds of paperwork are sales invoices and bills. Sales invoices are what you issue when you have sold work. Bills are what you receive when you have bought something or received services. Your invoice is someone's else's bill and vice versa - an electricity bill is the electricity company's invoice.

It is essential when selling work that a Sales Invoice be issued. However when work is being provided on 'sale-or-return' then no Sales Invoice can be issued until the work is actually sold. In such cases a sale-or-return record should be issued.

All paperwork which you issue should carry your name and address, telephone number and to whom cheques should be payable (if different).

A duplicate copy should be kept of all paperwork for your records. Include the date (the day posted) and number each type of document (delivery note, invoice, etc.) consecutively to help in your book-keeping and to guard against loss. To start numbering at 1 can have an amateur look so you may want to begin at 100 or 200 to make it appear that you have been trading for some time.

Stationers sell pads of invoices to which you can add your name and address, but it is better to have something which looks more professional and reflects the quality of the work you are selling. The simplest answer is to have a letterhead printed, stating who you are, your address and what you do which you can type on whatever document it is you are issuing.

Another approach is to have a multi-purpose form printed with your name, address and telephone number (and VAT number if registered) and along the top have listed the types of forms you need and score out when not relevant.

James Potter
32 Reading Lane
Newtown
01855 466543
Order Form / Delivery Note / Sale-or-Return Record / Invoice /
Credit Note

Note that if you are registered for VAT, there are certain other requirements and details can be obtained from your local VAT office.

Printing is relatively cheap, but the preparation of the original artwork can be expensive so it is worth doing it yourself or finding a friendly graphic artist to do it for you - maybe you can pay them with a piece of your work. If you do it yourself, use Letraset on white paper (A4 size is best) this will produce an adequate copy for an " instant printer" to use. Local print shops produce letterheads reasonably inexpensively, but make sure that the quality is good. Or you can have a rubber stamp made up with your letterhead.

Order Form

If you take an order at a gallery, craft fair, trade event, etc. then either obtain an order from the customer or issueone on their behalf. An order form should state the customer's name, their reference number if relevant, the quantity, price and description of goods ordered. Make sure they sign it and where you are writing it on their behalf give them a copy.

Delivery note

This accompanies goods you have sold, whether despatched or delivered. It should state the order number, customer's name, their reference if relevant, the quantity, price and description of goods delivered. If you deliver yourself, always get a signature on your copy as confirmation of receipt of the goods. If you are sending work by post it can be useful to make three copies, send two with the work and ask the customer to sign and return one copy of the delivery note as acknowledgement of the safe arrival.

If you are sending a mixed consignment, e.g. some of which has been purchased by the customer and some on sale-or-return, it is best to send a separate delivery note for the bought work and a sale-or-return record for the work supplied in consignment. This will help you keep track of which is which and assist you in raising your invoice.

Sale-or-return record or Consignment Note

If the work being delivered or sent is on saleorreturn then it is sensible to have a special form for the customer to sign to acknowledge that they have taken the work on sale-or-return. This should be dated, state the retailer's name, the quantity, description and price of each item. It should also contain the following clause to ensure that you can recover the work if it is unsold even if the gallery goes out of business. "Supplied on consignment, sale-or-return. The maker remains owner of the work until sold and the maker is paid in full."

In addition, as the shop/gallery is acting as your agent and therefore has no legal responsibility for work on sale-or-return while in their possession the following clause should be added : "(Name of outlet) shall reimburse the maker for any loss or damage to the goods from whatever cause while in their possession."

INVOICE

This is a request for payment and should be sent separately from the goods when you are supplying a firm, although with private clients or when delivering work yourself to a shop or gallery it can be handed over with the goods. It carries the same information including the number as the delivery note or sale orreturn record (remember that an "invoice " for goods left on sale-or-return is sent when the items, or part, have subsequently been sold), the total cost (plus VAT if applicable), any discounts and VAT number (where applicable).

It is worth adding the following sentence to invoice: "Payment due within 30 days. The maker remains owner of the work until payment is received in full."

This would ensure that you could take back work which you have sold but for which you are unpaid, in the event of the customer going out of business.

CREDIT NOTE

This should be issued if goods which have been purchased by a customer are returned for any reason. It is important that you keep a record of work returned otherwise there may be a dispute at a later stage as to whether you delivered the goods or not. When the returned goods are received, send the customer a credit note stating the order number, quantity, the type and price of each item, and the reason for return. If and when the goods are replaced, send a fresh invoice.

Where work which has been held on sale-or-return is returned then it is sensible to issue a note along the lines of the above Credit Note but stating that the work returned was held on sale-or-return. Again this helps keep track of who has possession of work.

STATEMENT

This is a reminder to the customer that he/she has not yet paid. It is usually issued when a month or so has elapsed since the invoice was sent and it is still unpaid. It quotes all outstanding unpaid invoices , totals them and deducts any credit notes issued. It is a way of politely pressing for payment. Where a discount has been offered for payment within a fixed period (say a month), as a statement is issued after the period is up the discount is removed.

Basic Book-keeping

There are several different systems of book-keeping:

THE "SHOE-BOX" SYSTEM

This is the simplest system. You need six filing (or shoe) boxes, a bank paying-in book, a cheque book, a small pad of receipts and a notebook.

The boxes should be labelled :

Box 1 Unpaid Invoices
Box 2 Paid Invoices
Box 3 Unpaid Bills
Box 4 Paid Bills
Box 5 Outstanding sale-or-return Records
Box 6 Receipts, etc.

When you issue a sales invoice put your copy in Box 1 (Unpaid Invoices). Then when you receive payment for that invoice take your copy from Box 1, mark on it the date payment was received and whether cash or by cheque, and transfer it to Box 2 (paid Invoices). Pay all cash and cheques received into the bank, recording the amounts in your paying-in book.

Similarly, when a bill comes in put it in Box 3 (Unpaid Bills). Then when you pay the bill take it from Box 3, write on it the date you paid it and the cheque number (or if it was cash) and transfer it to Box 4 (Paid Bills). Details of all cheques should be recorded on your cheque book stubs and in your Bank Book.

With this system it is important to check Box 3 regularly to make sure that bills have not been left unpaid after their final date. Otherwise you can find your telephone being cut off.

Also go through Box 1 at regular intervals and make sure none have been outstanding for too long. Unless you have agreed a longer payment period, it is worth sending out a statement after one month showing the amount outstanding as a reminder. If a statement has been sent and the invoice is still unpaid then start chasing.

Into Box 5 (Outstanding sale-or-return records) put your copies of sale-or-return records. When you hear that work which you have supplied on sale-or-return has been sold take the sale-or-return record from Box 5, write and send an invoice for the amount and mark on the sale-or-return record that you have issued an invoice. As the sale-or-return record will not be required by your accountant you can store it away.

Where only some of the work covered by the sale-or-return record has been sold then you should mark those items that have been sold, issue an invoice for those and return the sale-or-return record to Box 5 so that you have an on-going record of the remaining work still out on sale-or-return.

 Regularly look through Box 5 (Outstanding sale-or-return records) and check if any of the work on sale-or-return has been sold. Do not presume that in all cases the shop or gallery will inform you when they sell work which they have on sale-or-return.

Remember to keep an eye on any work which has been in a shop or gallery on sale-or-return too long. Work which is sitting in a gallery on sale-or-return has cost you money to produce.

When unsold work on sale-or-return is returned or collected mark if off against the relevant sale-or-return record and if that record is then finished with file away safely as mentioned above.

Box 6 (Receipts) is used to store all receipts for business expenditures. Whenever you incur an expense on the business you should try to obtain a receipt. Where you cannot get a receipt try to obtain some record of what was spent. Thus if it is bus or tube travel keep the ticket as the record of the expenditure. For other expenditure where you do not have a receipt or record use your small receipts book to note the amount, date and what the expenditure was so that you have a record.

Put all the receipts, tickets, notes on what has been spent, etc. in an envelope each week or month, mark on the front which period it relates to and put in Box 6.

Finally you should keep an account of all the amounts going in and out of your bank. This can be done by writing on your cheque stub but as there is likely to be a lot of entries it is better to record this in a simple Bank Book. For further information on running a simple accounts book ask your accountant or see ' Money Matters' (published by Artic Producers).

The above system is perfectly adequate if your turnover is small, and should enable you or your accountant to draw up annual accounts relatively simply.

Bought Book-keeping systems

While there are several book-keeping systems which can be purchased these tend to be complicated to run. While they come with full instructions and examples for each section, laid out ready for entries, the instructions are often difficult to follow. A further disadvantage is that none of them work unless they are kept up to date regularly, at least weekly and preferably daily. As a drawback this cannot be over-emphasised, for if they are allowed to get out of control it can cost even more in accountant's fees to sort them out!

Computer Book-keeping systems

There are a number of computer accounting programmes for small businesses and if you own or have regular access to a computer and are reasonably computer literate, it may be worth exploring one of these. However there is a danger if things go awry that it may be harder for your accountant to sort out your affairs. Thus you should take your accountant's advice if you are considering using a computer accounts package.

Given the range of software available it can be hard to know which might be most suitable. One that it is straightforward to use, reasonably priced and recommended by some people running small businesses is ' Money Manager'.

Employing a book-keeper

If you find doing the paperwork and book-keeping a chore, an answer could be to employ someone to undertake this work; a professional book-keeper will do it quicker and more effectively, and release you to do what you are best at - namely, designing and making. Often someone employed for even a few hours a week is sufficient. By advertising locally you may find a retired accountant or book-keeper who is interested in a few hours employment on a semi-regular basis.

Accounting for Value Added Tax (VAT)

If your annual turnover (not your profit or personal income) exceeds, or is likely to exceed, the declared level (£49,000 from 1 November 1998) then you are legally required to register with your local VAT office of the Customs and Excise.

It is possible to ask to be registered even if your turnover does not reach the declared level; this may be worth considering if you use expensive materials or if you export most of what you produce outside of the European Community as exports outside the EC are zero-rated.

As this book primarily is aimed at people setting up in business few will require to register for VAT and given the complexity of VAT, anyone wishing or requiring to become registered for VAT should take advice from an accountant.

For general information on VAT contact your local Customs and Excise VAT office. There is a general information leaflet - Should I be registerd for VAT? (Ref 700/1/92).

Business Bank Account

It is advisable to operate a separate bank account for your business; it will help you to keep your books and make it easier for your accountant to finalise your annual accounts. To begin with, you may just decide to open a number two bank account as a way of avoiding the higher bank charges normally levied on business accounts, but if you are doing substantial trading the bank is likely to notice and raise the charge accordingly. Therefore, it may be best to see your bank manager, explain that you are setting up your own crafts business but are unlikely to earn much in the first year or two, and to ask him/her to consider waiving the normal business service charges for an agreed period. Some banks offer free banking for a set period to people starting in business and it is worth checking to see if your bank runs such a scheme. An alternative might be to open a different bank account, say with a Building Society, and use that for your business.

RECONCILING YOUR BANK STATEMENT

You should arrange for bank statements to be sent to you monthly. When you receive each statement, check to see if there are any receipts (bank pay-ins, interest, etc.) or payments (cheques, direct debits, bank charges, etc.) which you have not yet included in your records and, if so, enter these in your bank account book. The next step is to reconcile the balance shown in your account book with that shown on the statement

Sub-contracting / employing staff

You may decide to have certain objects, or part of objects, made for you by someone else. This can be organised by employing staff or out-workers, or by sub-contracting work to another workshop or company. Or if an object sells particularly well, you might consider having it manufactured and sold by someone else under licence.

Clearly this decision can be sensible as it can enable you to produce more work or employ skills or technology you do not possess. However, you need to ensure that the quality of the final product is not impaired for it is this quality of making which you as a craftsperson, will be selling. If work is selling under your name, even if someone else is actually making part or all of it, you must exercise stringent quality control or your may start losing sales and/or reputation.

 Before employing anyone to undertake work for you, check their quality of making to ensure it meets your standard. You must also be careful that outworkers or sub-contractors deliver on time - crucial if you have contracted to produce work by a specific date as you will still be the person liable for late delivery.

OUTWORKERS/FREELANCERS/CASUAL HELP

There is a widespread but mistaken belief that by using outworkers or casual help no employer/employee relationship exists. The reality is that if you give them detailed instruction about what to do and how to do it then, in the eyes of the law, you may be seen to be employing them.

On the other hand there is no contract of employment, only a contract for services, if you have no control over their method of working.

For example, if you employ someone to make up your textiles into cushions and they work from their own home or workshop on their own equipment to their own hours and timescale and invoice you for the work, then they are sub-contractors and self-employed. However if they regularly come to your workshop and work on your equipment to your instructions then, in the eyes of the Inland Revenue, you are fairly certainly employing them whether payment is by a lump sum, a weekly wage, an hourly rate or for each piece produced.

This is an important point because, while no contract of employment need be issued, there are legal requirements covering tax and National Insurance and people employed regularly, whether as outworkers or freelancers, can be covered by other employment legislation if they are judged to be employees.

While the definition of employed / self-employed is fairly clear and the rules on tax and NI requirements explicit, many employers and casual outworkers are ignorant of them, or confused. Much of this confusion is encouraged by individuals who are knowingly evading tax, but be warned that to connive, knowingly or through ignorance, in such tax evasion can lead to trouble. The Inland Revenue is cracking down on this form of tax evasion and if it is discovered that you have been employing people without deducting and paying tax then you can be charged with all the tax that should have been paid.

Employees

If you are employing people, it is important to be aware of the requirements of the law; given the mass of employment legislation which now exists. You should contact your local Employment Office for advice and information. The Inland Revenue, in conjunction with the Benefits Agency publish "Information For Employers" CWG3 which will give you guidance on employing others.

Employing your husband or wife

You do not need to issue a spouse with a contract of employment, but again you are responsible for deducting tax and National Insurance where appropriate.

Sub-contracting

As has been explained above, sub-contracting is where you pass all or part of the making process to someone else for them to carry out in their workspace to their own timescale.

This can range from having some metal laser-cut by a large manufacturer to having another craftsperson make up your printed textiles into garments.

Selling under licence

Basically this is a process whereby you give someone the right to make and sell one of your designs in exchange for a fee and/or royalty. Given that most craft objects sell because they are individually made, this option will seldom be relevant, but it is worth considering where one of your objects is in great demand and could be mass-produced or produced on a limited basis by another manufacturer. The Chartered Society of Designers publish guides to royalty agreements, etc.

Insurance

With all matters of insurance, it is best to consult a qualified insurance broker who will be able to advise you on your needs and the cost. Insurance brokers do not charge for their services; instead they receive commission from the insurance companies.

The Association of British Insurers (ABI), 51 Gresham Street, London EC2V 7HQ (0171 600 3333) can help individuals and businesses by providing information about insurance. The ABI represents about 450 insurance companies which transact some 90% of insurance.

The following types of insurance should be considered:

Public Liability Insurance

If your workshop is visited by members of the public you should take out this insurance against any claims for injury or damage to third parties caused by your alleged negligence.

Motor Insurance

Check that your vehicle insurance covers your business activities.

Employers Liability Insurance

If you employ others, you are legally required to take out this insurance.

Fire & Theft Insurance

You should insure your workshop, equipment and stock. If you are working from home you must check to see if your home insurance is invalidated by your workshop activity or you will be in danger of having any claims refused. Check to see if your insurance covers equipment or tools when not on the premises; for example working on a commission on site.

Goods in Transit Insurance

This may be worth considering to cover work if you regularly transport expensive items.

Personal Accident Insurance

If you are injured or become ill you may have to give up work for a time which would result in loss of income and personal accident insurance would provide an income; particularly important if you have dependants.

Product Liability Insurance

If you make work which is potentially dangerous in use, such as furniture or lighting, then you may wish to investigate this type of insurance.

Telephone

With new companies such as Mercury entering the market it is worth investigating what is on offer to see if you can find a deal that will save you money. What is best may depend on the type and/or time of calls you make.

Check the rates for different times of the day and limit outgoing calls to the least expensive times when possible. Also try and keep calls short.

 It is important that people can contact you by telephone and an answering machine will ensure that people can at least leave a message. Prospective customers are likely to fade away if after two or three attempts to phone you they do not get through. Another advantage of an answering machine is that it cuts down interruptions while you are working. The disadvantages of answering machines are that some people dislike leaving messages on them, although this is probably less so now given their wide use, and that you can end up paying more in outgoing calls phoning back. However, on balance they are a help to any small business where it is not feasible to have someone available to answer the phone all the time.

Organising your time

Organising your time can be difficult given the range of tasks to be done and the sudden demands and crises which require urgent attention. But it is essential that you exercise some control or you will find yourself rushing from one thing to another in a fragmented way. In Chapter 1 we suggested preparing an action plan and this can be a useful method of assisting you to plan the most effective use of your time. By keeping a check on this, you can guard against the natural inclination to put off doing things which you do not want to do. By planning you can focus on particular aspects of your work and business.

If you are working under pressure there is a tendency to respond to each new demand instantly, when in fact this is often unnecessary. Placing tasks in order of priority will help counteract this and assist in keeping to essential deadlines.

Given that the cost of work is related to the hours spent making, the first priority is to ensure that making time does not fall below a set number of hours each working week. The second priority is to give sufficient time to selling and promoting your work; you should allocate a specific amount of time per week or month as a minimum.

It can be helpful to keep a strict record of how your time is spent for a week or two, as an experiment. This will show the actual situation, which may be quite different from what you believe to be the case. You will be able to see the percentage of time spent on making, administration, selling, etc., and if the balance is wrong consider how best to adjust your pattern of working.

Although it is important not to waste working time, you should not be worried if you spend an hour chatting to the maker next door or sketching the view in the park. You are your own boss and if you have worked fourteen hours the day before, then some time off the next may be just the break you need to keep you effective and contented. There is little point in being a craftsperson and working long hours for little cash if you do not get satisfaction from the life. It is difficult to retain integrity about your work and be creative if you stop enjoying yourself.

One way to help ease your time problems is to employ people to do the things you are not good at. Part-time help for simple labouring tasks may be cost-effective in terms of your time saved. Colleges are often keen to place students temporarily for work experience.

Another way to ease time problems is to pool tasks with other makers. It may be that there are three makers in your area, all of whom are regularly visiting the same outlets to deliver work or going to the same place to buy materials, and some form of "pool" system could save everyone time and money. Such co-operation could extend to attending craft fairs where a stand could be jointly hired and staffed, or to joint publicity, so that everyone's limited resources can be stretched further. Guilds and societies are well placed to initiate such co-operation and many already do, so check to see if this is a good reason for joining the one relevant to your work or area.

66 Finding a solicitor

Most small businesses will need a solicitor sooner or later, but, unlike an accountant who will hopefully keep a watchful eye on the business month by month, a solicitor is generally employed for a specific purpose. Services do not come cheaply but for certain purposes it is foolish not to use them; the results of DIY legal drafting can be very expensive indeed if a legal battle arises. The most obvious areas for caution are buying or leasing property, forming a partnership or limited company, or making a will. However, solicitors are often a mine of information and advice and it is as well to make contact with a suitable firm fairly early on in the life of your business.

As with accountants, the best way to find a good solicitor is by personal recommendation. However, most solicitors specialise to some extent and you should not assume that the solicitor who dealt with the transfer of your friend's house will necessarily be prepared to act for you in taking action against a gallery which refuses to pay. Even if they are prepared to act, they may not be as efficient as a firm which specialises in this area of work. An alternative source of recommendation is to write to The Law Society, 113 Chancery Lane, London WC2 and ask for a list of solicitors in your county; this list sets out the specialities of each practice and grades them A, B or C according to the volume of work they handle in each area. They also run a scheme "Lawyers for Enterprise" which offers a free consultation on legal matters. The first session will indicate the help that can be given and estimate the cost.

Generally speaking, smaller crafts business should avoid the very large firms where the fees may be higher and the partners too busy to consider your affairs. Instead go for the small to medium sized firm in the nearest large town, where you can build up a personal relationship over the years.

A detailed reference book on the laws relating to small business is Croner's Reference Book for the Self-Employed and Smaller Business. The book is updated monthly on a loose-leaf system and a regularly updated copy is available in the Crafts Council's Library for reference.

Making a will

As a postscript to this chapter it is appropriate to remind you to make a will, especially if you have dependants or assets. Admittedly, making a will will not make running your workshop and business any easier, but it may bring a little peace of mind in the knowledge that if you die the legal process of sorting out your business affairs and assets will be more straightforward, and probably more beneficial, for those you leave behind. A solicitor will not charge much more to draw up a will than the cost of a modest meal for two, and the effect lasts rather longer.

Workspace

 Choosing a workspace will depend on a variety of factors – your personal preferences, what you can afford, the types of workshop available, etc. – and you will probably have to settle for a space that does not meet all your requirements. Before even beginning to look for a workshop, make a checklist of your requirements and put them in order of importance. Then if you find a workspace that meets, say the top five, you can decide to take it. Be careful not to end up in a workshop that is too small or too depressing. You will probably spend more time in your workshop than at home, so it is important to have a space that is relatively pleasant to be in; if the space is too restricted or grim, your work is likely to suffer.

Working from home

Technically anyone operating a business from their home needs to have planning permission. However as long as your craft activity is not changing the character of the property e.g. by making major internal alterations or having lots of customers visit you or creating fumes or noise you will not need to worry. If in doubt or if you do think you need to seek planning permission, contact the planning department of your local council and tell them what you propose; they will inform you if there are any restrictions and how these can be met. Planning authorities have been instructed to assist small businesses in setting up and you should find them helpful, especially if you ask their advice in good time rather than after you have started.

You must check with your local council if you plan to regularly employ other people in the workshop, make alterations to the building, use noisy machinery or dangerous chemicals, or have lots of people visiting to buy work.

You should also take account of your tenancy agreement, lease or mortgage. Where would you stand with your insurance company or building society, for example, if there was a fire resulting from your business activities? By working from home you may be breaking the terms of such agreements, which could lead to their termination if you have not obtained permission. Insurance policies are issued on the basis that you provide all relevant information, so if you work from home without informing the insurance company you could be in danger of nullifying your policy. If you are not increasing the risks (by using volatile chemicals, machinery, etc.) informing them should not materially affect the premium you have to pay.

If you are working from home and the property is classified as 'residential' you do not have to pay Business Rates (the Unified Business Rate). You merely pay your Council Tax.

Renting a workshop

If you decide to rent a space outside the home, there are two alternatives: to rent space in a group workshop or an individual workshop.

GROUP WORKSHOPS

The Crafts Council has a list of group workshops throughout the country, available free on request. There are two main types of group workshop. One involves the workshop being open to the public, either for all or part of the time. Some of these offer rents which are less than the normal commercial rental. All normally offer the opportunity for selling direct to the public. Whether or not such a situation appeals to you will tend to depend on your ability and wish to work with the public looking on. You should take account of the fact that interruptions will tend to reduce the amount of time available for making. Also you will need to consider if the type of people visiting the centre are likely to want to buy your work.

 Other group workshops are developments where a building contains a number of units, not open to the public. These are particularly popular as they combine the advantages of your own workshop and contact with people working in similar disciplines. Working on your own can be difficult, especially when things are not going well, and a group workshop offers the chance to exchange ideas and share problems. Some group workshops offer central services such a secretarial help, book-keeping and a selling/ gallery space. Group workshops offer the additional advantage in that buyers can visit several makers at one time.

The group can combine to organise promotional activities, for instance, Red Herring Workshops in Brighton have held exhibitions of past and present members' work, and Cockpit Arts in London holds events where the workshops are open to the public for a period once a year. This is a particularly good way of encouraging new buyers and journalists to visit.

Some craftspeople have found good workshops by looking for an empty building that would be suitable, discovering who is responsible for it and offering to make it usable as workspaces for a rent-free period or low rent. A number of local councils are interested in assisting with the development of such projects as they can be beneficial for employment and tourism. If you are a member of a group of craftspeople interested in developing a group workshop or know of a building that might be possible to use for group workshops you should contact your Regional Arts Board for advice on how you might take the idea forward.

Individual workshop

By far the best way of finding a workshop is by word of mouth, so let as many people as possible know you are looking.

Advertisements are another good source of information – local newsagents, 'CRAFTS' magazine and 'ARTISTS NEWSLETTER' usually have details of space available. Your local council may be able to help you and some have lists of property for rent, but you should be prepared to wait a few weeks as the wheels tend to grind slowly in council departments. Again check with your Regional Arts Board.

It may be worth combining with others looking for space and finding somewhere to rent jointly. Some areas of the country offer special assistance to those needing small workshops and it is worth consulting your local council's small business division for information. The Rural Development Commission also produces a list of workshops it has available.

POINTS TO CONSIDER WHEN CHOOSING A WORKSPACE

What part of the country should you choose? Should it be an urban or a rural area? You will need to think about your market; if you have to travel miles to deliver work, this could prove costly. Alternatively, if you are hoping people will come to you, you must be sure you are accessible – a mile down a bumpy track may deter potential customers! Think about your neighbours; if you are selling direct to the public, will a constant stream of customers (at least in the summer) cause a problem?

How much can you afford? Find out whether the rent you have been quoted includes rates, and if not find out how much they are as in some places they can often work out more expensive than the rent. Rents are often expressed in cost per square foot per year, for example, studio size 20 x 16 ft @ £6 per sq. ft. will cost £1,920 per annum, or about £38 per week. And are you responsible for any repairs?

 Does the rent include heating and lighting, and any other services, such as secretarial help? If it does do you really need these other services? Try and find out how much all your overheads are likely to be.

Is the space the right size? You do not want to be paying for space you are not using. On the other hand, you may want to allow for some expansion or additional equipment in the future.

What else is essential for the sort of work you do? For instance, do you need a good source of natural light? If you are using heavy machines, you must ensure that the floors are strong enough to take their weight, and if you use a loom a high ceiling may be required. If you need to bring in a large item of machinery, will you be able to get it through a door or window?

What sort of electricity supply does the workshop have? Some equipment requires three-phase, which is expensive to install and in some places unavailable. Do you need gas? Is water available? A telephone is essential for running any sort of business; if one is not already installed, it is costly to have this done and may take time. How will you heat the workshop? Are there any restrictions about using portable gas or paraffin heaters, which can be dangerous?

Are there any restrictions on the use of certain types of equipment or materials? Are the fire precautions in the workshop adequate? Think about the potential hazards – the use of chemicals or spraying equipment. Is this likely to cause any problems, for you or neighbours? Is there good ventilation? This is particularly important if you will be creating dust or fumes.

What restrictions are there on access? Can you use the workshop only at certain hours, and what about weekends? If you have a rush job to do, this could be vital. Are there any conditions linked to the space, such as having to open to the public at certain times? Is the workshop secure?

Think about relationships with the landlord and other tenants. Will you have to sign a lease or licence? (A lease gives you more security of tenure but many workshops are now offered by licence agreement.) If so, it is worth considering the length of the lease. For those starting up their first workshop a short, renewable lease is probably best. Discover who is responsible for maintenance and repairs. Usually the landlord will deal with anything external or communal, and you will be responsible for internal repairs to your own space. Make sure you have some form of written agreement. If you are sharing a workshop with others, make sure you are clear about what the arrangements are concerning ownership of and sale of equipment, use of joint facilities such as the telephone, and payment of bills. Again, it is best to have something in writing. You may think you are good friends but disputes over sharing can all too easily arise.

Finally, be certain that the space is one you will be happy working in. Given that you are likely to spend long hours there, a dark, damp space, which seems a bargain because of its low rent, may turn out to be a bad investment if you begin to find it depressing.

Workspace

76 SCHEDULING YOUR MOVE

Once you decide on premises, it may be useful to make a list of the things which need doing before you can start production and the dates by which these should be completed. For example:

WEEK ONE
– Move in
– Install three-phase electricity
– Repair roof
– Arrange connection of telephone

WEEK TWO
– Decorate
– Have equipment delivered and connected
– Build shelves

WEEK THREE
– Have materials delivered
– Organise work space

WEEK FOUR
– Start production

Equipment

List the essential equipment you require to start making. While it may be possible to get under way without everything you need, by borrowing equipment or using facilities elsewhere, you must be careful that such a situation will not lead to problems in fulfilling orders. For example, firing your work in someone else's kiln or at your old college can serve to test out the market but is unlikely to be satisfactory in the long term. Obtaining the essential equipment before you start is almost certainly going to make your business more efficient and reduce problems.

Research the different types of equipment and the availability of good second-hand equipment. It is worth asking others working at your craft for their recommendations or criticisms. Also think hard about the size or power – easy to believe you are saving money by buying a cheaper version, only to discover after a short while that it is too small or under-powered. When buying equipment, you must imagine your developing needs over a number of years and balance that against your available funds and the likely space you will have in your workshop. Be careful of getting equipment which is much larger than you really need or borrowing a lot of money to buy equipment that is not essential. For example, too large a kiln can hold up production, limit experimentation and cause major financial problems if a kiln load goes wrong. Equally, over-committing yourself financially to buy non-essential equipment can force you into doing work you would rather not do just to repay the loan.

Legal points

Landlord and tenant law, workshop leases and tenancy agreements

You will need to instruct a solicitor to act for you in settling the exact terms of a lease or tenancy agreement, but it is as well if you can sort out the major terms at an early stage in the negotiations.

First what is the length of the lease and the rent, and can the rent be raised ("reviewed") during the term? If the lease is for more than three years, almost certainly the landlord will retain the right to raise the rent in line with market values. Next, you should check who is responsible for repairing the premises. The normal arrangement on a shortish lease is for the landlord to agree to carry out external repairs, including structural work, the roof and drains, while the tenant becomes responsible for internal repairs, including the glass in the windows. On a short lease you might be responsible for internal decorations only, while on a long lease you may have to undertake all repairs. The exact wording of the repair clause can be crucial and your solicitor will advise.

Thirdly, if you want to share your premises or split it up amongst a number of people, will the landlord allow you to sub-let part of the premises?

Finally, if you wish to leave the workshop before the end of the lease, will you be allowed to transfer the remainder of it to someone else? If not, you may find yourself paying for premises you no longer want.

Planning permission, bye-law approval, fire regulations

For the purposes of the planning regulations, crafts are classed as "light industry" and you should check with the local authority that the workshop you propose to rent has the necessary planning permission. If it does not, you will have to apply for permission. This can be a long, drawn-out process but it is usually possible to obtain an informal opinion fairly quickly as to the likely outcome of an application from the planning officer at the local authority.

If you intend to alter the building, again you may need planning permission, but almost certainly you will also have to comply with Building Regulations as well.

Finally, and especially if you intend to employ others, the premises must comply with fire regulations. More potential workshops have never got off the ground for this single reason than for any other.

Business Rates

The Unified Business Rate is charged on all work premises and this charge is tax deductible. Note that if you are working from home you will just pay your Community Charge and not the Unified Business Rate unless the workshop part of your home has been designated as non-domestic premises.

Costing and Pricing

Costing is the term used to calculate the price an object costs to produce. In all manufacturing, costing is a crucial tool in ensuring that the business is not selling work at a loss and thereby going bust. The cost price also assists in the setting of the selling price of the finished object although the link between the cost and selling price is complex. In normal commercial business the one golden rule is that work should never be sold at less than cost price. It may be that the selling price is far in excess of the cost price. For example a shirt sold in a fashionable shop at £65 may have cost little more to produce than one selling in a high street store for £25. The maxim for setting the selling price could be best described as you sell at what the market can bear.

However for many craft businesses costing and pricing are problematic areas and the golden rule that work should never be sold for less than it cost to produce is often broken. In reality craftspeople often make work which costs more to produce than it can sell for in the market place. Thus a ceramicist may spend weeks working on a sculptural piece and calculate the cost price to be £2,000. However such a price may be unrealistic in the market in which that type of work sells and the maker may have to accept that £500 is a more realistic selling price. If the maker is unwilling to compromise the quality of the making and wishes to sell, then he/she may need to accept a selling price of £500, thereby making a loss.

The reason that this is a factor within the crafts is that many craftspeople are not working to a specific market. Rather they are working to their own creative agenda and so are willing to accept the reality that their work may not sell at the price it should.

Yet the situation varies between crafts and craftspeople. While some work sells at a loss, other work is produced which sells at a profit; some craftspeople have to subsidise their business with other employment;

others are able to sell their work at prices far above the cost price and live off their making.

Costing

While for many craftspeople the cost price may not relate to the actual selling price it is important that all craftsmen and women try to calculate, at least roughly, the cost price of their objects.

Such costing can assist in setting the selling price although it may not be the final factor. Knowing what your work should sell for can assist in the success of your workshop business, for if you are to survive you must either cover the costs of the workshop and earn enough to live on or recognise that you are going to have to subsidise your business through other earnings.

The myriad of approaches and markets in the crafts makes it difficult to create a costing system which is relevant to the production of all crafts. Thus the method suggested here can only be a guide but it may be helpful in assisting you to work out, even if only approximately, costings for your work.

If you share the workshop, then of course some of your overheads will be shared and you should adjust the annual cost accordingly.

To calculate what your work costs, you need to consider four ingredients: overheads, labour, materials and contingency/profit.

Workshop/Business Overheads

These are all the cost of running your workshop and business, which have to be paid whether or not you are making work. Overheads can be divided into four headings.

 WORKSHOP EXPENSES include bills directly connected with running the workspace, such as rent or mortgage repayment, electricity, gas, cleaning, maintenance and repairs, etc. If your workspace is in your house, include a relevant percentage of the bills.

BUSINESS EXPENSES include those bills which, although not directly linked to the workspace, are essential parts of running your business, such as postage, travelling/motor car expenses, photography, advertising, craft fair fees, insurance, accountant's fee, etc.

EQUIPMENT/LOANS If you have bought equipment, an amount to cover the replacement cost should be included – this is called depreciation. Reflect the expected life of the equipment by dividing the cost by the number of years which you expect the equipment to last, for example, £1,000 equipment expected to last five years should be charged at £200 each year (£1,000÷5). The reason for making this depreciation charge is that you will hopefully make a profit and have cash in the bank when the time comes to replace the equipment. As regards loans connected with the business (for equipment or starting-up capital), the cost of the annual repayments and interest charges must also be included.

STOCK If you keep stocks of raw materials these will cost you money just sitting on the shelf as you will have to pay for them initially, probably by borrowing money. If the stock is precious metal or expensive components, this can amount to a lot of money. To cover this, at least 20% of the average stock value should be added to the overheads, in addition to any loan/overdraft costs.

To work out the first element of your costing, you need to estimate what your annual overheads will be or have been in previous years. Clearly, with so many different things to take into account, everyone's overheads will be very different and the example below is merely to provide a working model.

EXAMPLE: ANNUAL OVERHEADS OF A SMALL WORKSHOP

	£
Rent/rates	2,420
Gas and electricity	500
Maintenance and repairs	120
Cleaning materials	80
Telephone	360
Motor expenses, parking, etc.	650
Postage and stationery	90
Photography and advertising	200
Craft fair fees	480
Accountant	190
Insurance	260
Loan interest/repayments	210
Stock (20% of £400)	80
Equipment (£600 over 5 years)	120
Total	5760

Thus, in our example it costs £5,760 to run the workshop over a year. The next step is to calculate this annual cost as an hourly rate. First divide by the number of weeks worked in the year. (Do not forget to give yourself holidays!). Base your costing on, say, a 48 week year. Divide the annual cost by the number of working weeks. In our example this would be £5,760 divided by 48 weeks, which works out at £120 per week.

The next step is to work out the number of hours in each week actually spent making. It is important to remember that, as well as your making hours, your working week will include time spent on paperwork, selling, answering the phone, travelling, business correspondence, etc. and that this time must somehow be charged. The simplest way is to calculate the percentage of time in an average week you spend actually making. "Making" means all the activity directly related to producing the craft object. For our example, let us presume that 60% of the time is actually spent making. A point to note is that the less time you spend making, the more you will have to charge for what you produce, and that if you end up spending too little time making, your cost price will rise dramatically.

Having calculated the percentage of time spent making, we can now calculate an hourly rate. For this calculation, base it on a 40-hour week. You will probably work a lot more than 40 hours, but if you cost your work on the basis of an 60 hour week you will have to work 60 hours every week to survive. Whereas by basing your costing on a 40 hour week then when you work more hours you should make extra profit. In our example we reckon to spend 60% of the time making. On the basis of a 40-hour week that means 24 hours (60% of 40) each week are spent making.

We calculated the weekly overheads to be £120. If we divide this by the making hours in the week (which we have worked out to be 24), this gives us the hourly overhead rate of £5 (120÷24).

Okay so far? Good. Now let us look at the other ingredients.

LABOUR (YOUR EARNINGS)

This is what you want to earn. You will know roughly what you need to pay all your personal bills and live on. The simplest way to calculate an hourly labour cost is to decide how much you would hope to earn in the year. In self-employment, you do not receive a wage. Instead, as you go along you take money out of the business (cash drawings). For this example, let's presume we need £7,200 a year to live on. We have already decided to calculate on the basis of a 48-week year. So again we divide the annual sum by the working weeks to give a weekly charge (£7,200÷ 48 = £150 a week). To work out the hourly rate which needs to be charged to ensure that you earn your £7,200 a year, again divide the weekly charge by the making hours, which in our example we have already calculated to be 24 hours. Thus the hourly labour rate is £6.25 (£150÷24).

Materials

These are straightforward. You charge to each object the cost of the raw materials used in its production. If you are making a batch of objects, you simply divide the total cost by the number of objects to give the material cost per object.

Contingency

This is another simple calculation. Once you have worked out the object cost, taking into account the overheads, labour and materials, a flat percentage is added to cover such unknowns as breakages, unexpected bills, etc. At best it may also mean that you make a little more than your hoped-for basic earnings. The flat percentage might, for example, be 15%; perhaps less on higher-priced objects.

Having worked out the hourly overheads and labour rates, all you now need to calculate is how long an object takes to make to do the final costing. As examples, let us look at the production of a pottery jug and a silver bracelet.

COSTING OF JUG

Let us presume that on average it takes 40 minutes to make four jugs, 20 minutes to glaze and decorate them and 20 minutes as a proportion of the time spent firing the kiln. Therefore the making time for one jug is 20 minutes (80 minutes÷4).

Overheads 1/3 (20 minutes) of hourly rate @ £5	1.66
Labour 1/3 (20 minutes) of hourly rate @ £6.25	2.10
Materials	.80
Making price	4.56
Contingency/profit (15%)	.69
Cost price of jug (excluding any VAT)	5.25

COSTING OF BRACELET

Let us presume that it takes 16 hours to make the bracelet.

Overheads 16 hours @ £5	80.00
Labour 16 hours @ £6.25	100.00
Materials (silver)	35.60
Making price	215.60
Contingency/profit (10%)	21.50
Cost price of bracelet (excluding any VAT)	237.10

Discount

This is a reduction in price offered to encourage quicker payment. Even small discounts can encourage customers to pay promptly and many shops pay out first on invoices that carry a discount. However, do not offer a discount unless you have adjusted your price. If a 10% discount is being offered for repayment within one month of delivery you need to add on 1/9th of the basic selling (wholesale) price thus:

	Wholesale price	1/9th to take account of discount	Revised wholesale price
Jug	£ 10.25	£ 1.15	£ 11.40
Bracelet	£285.00	£31.65	£316.65

Thus, if the bill is settled promptly, you will receive your basic wholesale price, whereas if the customer is slow to pay you receive an extra amount to compensate you for the delay.

Bracelet	£316.65
less 10% discount if settled within 30 days	£31.65
Discounted price	£285.00

Costing for commissions

Costing for commissions is basically the same, except that you will have to estimate the time it will take and the cost of materials in advance. Given that it is all too easy to under-estimate these and so end up making a loss, be careful and, if anything, over-estimate. If in the end it takes less time, then that will mean more profit. Also remember to charge for the design time.

When calculating what materials you require, allow for wastage and be aware of the quantities in which you may have to order. You may have to buy or hire special tools. These are all costs which should be charged into the final price.

Establish carefully any items, such as VAT, which are based on a rate which may change. If you are liable for VAT, always give figures exclusive of VAT, stating this is so.

You may incur other incidental expenses. You may have to make site visits, attend planning meetings or undertake special research. If you are working with other people such as architects, you may have to consult them frequently. Should they happen to be in America, your telephone bill could be spectacular! You should itemise additional expenses beyond any usual reasonable workshop costs, which the client may then agree to pay as chargeable extras.

In setting a sum for contingencies, remember that things can always go wrong. Don't forget that you may have to make special arrangements for delivery and, unless they are to be charged separately, you must include these costs in the price.

If you are confident in the accuracy of your costing, having made suitable allowance for unforeseen eventualities, you can submit a quotation to your client rather than an estimate. This might be an important "selling point" in convincing the client that the commission should go ahead, since there will be no additional costs. But be careful as you will have to carry the cost of any overspending.

While there is no hard-and-fast legal definition of a "quote" or "estimate", it is generally agreed that a "quote/quotation" is a firm commitment to produce the object at the price stated, whereas an “estimate” is merely a fair guess and allows for flexibility in the final price.

A safer course if you are unsure of certain factors in the costing is to give some parameters (not more than £x and not less than £y).

With experience, knowing how and what to charge becomes easier. It never becomes less important. No matter how good the design and execution of your work, if you cannot get your costing right you may either lose money, which can be painful, or lose business by being seen to be expensive. Experience of analysing each commission will improve the accuracy of your estimating, helping you to compete without being unprofitable.

Costing of commissioned table

For this example we will combine the two rates for overheads (£5) and labour (£6.25) to give an hourly rate of £11.25.

Therefore for an initial design which you reckon will take 12 hours you would charge a fee of £135 (12 x £11.25).

If you had to make a special site visit or other journeys linked to the commission you would charge the hourly rate plus travel.

Making of table

Although with most commissions the timescale is probably days or weeks rather than hours, you still use the same method. In our example of 24 making hours a week if you think the commission would take two days to make then you would cost at 10 hours (roughly 5 making hours per day x 2) or if two weeks then 48 hours (2 weeks at 24 making hours per week).

 Thus for a table you estimate will take just over two weeks to make you might add a couple of days to be safe and base your estimate on three weeks working. As has already been said, with commissions it pays to be over-cautious when estimating the time it will take to make.

Overheads & labour (3 weeks):	
72 hours @ £11.25	810.00
Materials	65.00
	875.00
Contingency (10%)	87.50
Cost price of table (excluding any VAT)	£962.50

Thus you might charge an initial design fee of £135 and estimate the cost to be not less than £1000 and not more than £1,200. When it came to the final quote you might state £ 980 exclusive of VAT.

Setting the selling price

Working out the cost price is a first step in guiding you on setting a selling price. However the cost price will seldom be the price at which you sell. As was stated in the introduction to this chapter the maxim for setting the price is to sell for what the market will bear.

While craftspeople might wish it to be otherwise, the truth is that generally craft objects sell at the price the market is prepared to pay. Factors such as reputation, fashion, colour, material, media coverage, etc. are as likely to affect the price as the skill and creativity which has gone into producing it.

Also customers' perceptions of price vary between crafts. An object of similar scale and making time produced in glass will probably sell for more than one made of ceramic, while in certain crafts the market is so under-developed objects may only be saleable at less than the cost of production.

Many craftsmen and women are concerned that their work costs as much as it does. However, given that craft objects are unique objects and few craftspeople get very rich from their craft, this concern seems misplaced. When you have to employ an electrician or get your car fixed, the hourly rate you will be charged will be far greater than the one most craftspeople charge. Yet craftsmen and women have special skills, normally the result of many years' training, and you should not be afraid to ask for a reasonable return for these skills.

It has to be said that many craftspeople are schizophrenic about their selling price; one part feels that their work deserves to sell for a far higher price, given the skill and creativity involved, while the other part worries that the work is costing too much, often because the maker's economy is poorer than that of the customer.

Many craftspeople find that they can sell everything they make, yet resist charging more. If you are able to sell everything you make, it is likely that you are setting your selling price too low. Try raising your price and see what happens. Many craftspeople are working 80 hours a week and selling everything they make. If they doubled their prices and as a result demand was halved, they would actually earn as much while only working 40 hours a week.

As your business develops, you should be looking to be earning more from your skills and it is not unreasonable to decide that £10,000 a year rather than £6,000 is what you want to earn and charge accordingly.

 Market forces determine the price work can be sold for and you should not be afraid to increase your prices if the market will stand it.

Thus while knowing the cost price of your work is important, setting the selling price will be affected by a range of factors. Two of particular importance to craftwork are :

– The prices for similar work in your craft area.
– The context in which the work is selling.

PRICING WITHIN YOUR CRAFT AREA

If you make work that is similar to others in your field and which sells in the same network then there will be a scale of selling prices within which you will have to fit. For example a jeweller producing silver earrings and selling them through craft galleries is unlikely to be able to sell them for more than similar earrings produced by a maker with a greater reputation. Thus in arriving at your selling price you will need to research the prices of equivalent work.

This need to set your price within the context of the particular market can be the same even if you are not selling your work through normal retail craft outlets. If you were exhibiting your work in a fine art gallery you might set your price in relation to other work within the exhibition or if you were selling a large piece by commission to a corporate client by what they would pay for similar scale work in other mediums.

It has to be said that where there is little or no equivalent work on which a price scale can be based, such as an unusual commission, then you will need to make your best judgement. In such cases, particularly if the price is going to be substantial, it is worth being bold in setting a price. While you can always negotiate the price down it is almost impossible to negotiate it up.

CONTEXT IN WHICH THE WORK IS SELLING

The context in which work is selling also affects the final selling price. As has been mentioned before, clothes selling in a top fashion shop may not have cost much more to produce than those in Marks & Spencer but the fashionable label will mean a far higher mark-up. Similarly, a ceramic bowl sitting on a trestle table at a local craft fair will be unlikely to fetch as high a price as the same piece beautifully exhibited in an established gallery.

So you must think hard about all these points before deciding on your selling price. One factor that affects quite a lot of craft pricing is that craftspeople's economies are seldom strong and therefore makers often think that the price they have set is too high when in fact for customers with higher levels of earnings the price may seem more than fair.

The other important point to be aware of is that there can be different selling prices depending on the method of selling the work. We will now look at the normal ways of setting the selling price in the main selling situations.

SELLING TO SHOPS

If you are selling direct to shops or galleries then you will normally be selling the work at a WHOLESALE PRICE or TRADE PRICE. The shop or gallery then adds its mark-up to cover its costs. This will normally result in a RETAIL PRICE to the customer of double or more the cost price.

For example, a piece of work for which you decide you wish to receive £85 (your wholesale price) selling through an outlet with a 100% mark-up would have a retail price of £170 (plus VAT if you and/or the outlet were VAT registered).

 Some craftspeople feel that shop/gallery mark-ups are unfair but you need to recognise that the shop/gallery must cover its own costs if it is to survive. And if the shop sells your work on a regular basis, this will free you from many of the problems of marketing your work and thereby release more of your time for making.

If the shop/gallery is taking your work on a sale-or-return basis, then you may wish to negotiate for the mark-up to be less than if the outlet was buying the work outright. In such instances you should adjust your wholesale price accordingly so that the retail price in the outlet is the same. Thus your higher wholesale price compensates for the fact that you are taking the risk rather than the outlet.

SELLING THROUGH EXHIBITIONS

The usual practice is for you to set, or agree with the gallery, the price the work will sell for in the exhibition (again the 'retail price') and for the gallery to take a commission on the sale. In effect the gallery is acting as your agent.

It is important to know in advance the gallery's normal commission. Let us look at the example of the piece of work for which your wholesale price is normally £85 which is to be exhibited in gallery A which takes a 40% commission and gallery B which takes 50%.
The simplest way is to start from what you want the price to be to the customer. As a general rule you should try to ensure that the retail price of your work is similar in all selling situations.

Thus you set the price in the exhibition (exclusive of any VAT) at £170 (what it would sell for in an outlet with a 100% mark-up). Gallery A would take £ 68 commission (40% of £170) and you would receive £102 whereas with Gallery B you would receive £ 85 as their commission would be £85 (50% of £170).

If you are having to pay some of the costs of the exhibition then you should expect the gallery's commission to be reduced to take account of these costs.

Selling direct to the public from the workshop

If you normally sell through shops and only occasionally sell to the public, then charge the public close to the normal shop retail price. This has two advantages. First, it stops the shops from feeling that you are undercutting them (a feeling that could lead to them refusing to stock your work) and, second, it means more profit for you. A small discount of say 20% over the shop price would normally be acceptable.

If you sell most of what you produce direct from your workshop, then it is up to you to decide what to charge. Visits by the public to your workshop will interrupt your making, so it is certainly worth taking this into account when setting the selling price.

Selling through craft fairs

The same guidelines apply as selling direct from the workshop. If you also sell through retail outlets sell at, or close to, the normal retail price. If you only sell through craft fairs then it is up to you to set the price.

Some craft fairs, such as Chelsea Craft Fair, can involve selling direct to the public and taking orders from retail outlets. In such cases you will need to have two prices. The wholesale price for orders or sales to outlets and a retail price for direct sales to the public. Never display the wholesale price at such events. Display the retail prices and have your wholesale prices on a sheet which you can give to bona fide gallery/shop owners. Also be wary of requests for one or two objects at the wholesale price from shops or gallery owners as this may be them wanting a cheaper deal for themselves. Minimum orders (twenty objects or £200) at the wholesale price is a useful way of guarding against this.

98 SELLING BY COMMISSION
If you are commissioned to make something specially then it is up to you to set the price. The important thing with commissions is to discuss the price at an early stage to avoid confusion or misunderstanding.

Market resistance

When people start saying they think your work is over-priced, the temptation is to lower the price. As an excuse for selling at less than cost price, many makers say that they are only doing it temporarily to encourage further sales in the future. While this can, in exceptional cases, be a valid reason, you have to be careful not to get into a situation where the buyer will always expect to buy at that price level.

As much craft work involves many hours of work, objects can appear expensive in comparison with mass produced items, and there may well be market resistance to your work on the grounds of its price. If this is an issue you may need to address it. But, before doing so, stop and consider if price is the real problem. When work does not sell, a common reaction by the maker is to presume that the reason is that the work is thought too expensive but further investigation may show it is other factors. However, if there is market resistance due to price and you wish to continue to sell your work you will need to consider how to resolve the point.

TRY OTHER MARKETS. It may be that one selling outlet believes that the object is over-priced, while another might think the price reasonable. Similarly, a different clientele may have other views on what the object is worth.

TRY SELLING IT FOR MORE RATHER THAN LESS. Believe it or not, there are makers who have found that certain objects which will not sell at one price will sell really well at an even higher price! Somehow those buying the object perceive it to be worth more.

CUT DOWN ON YOUR OVERHEADS. This is not always possible, but it is worth examining your workshop and business bills to see if any savings can be made. If your workshop is large or only partly used, then sharing it with someone else could help reduce the cost to you.

INCREASE THE INHERENT VALUE. By using more expensive materials or improving the quality it is often possible to increase the selling price by far more than the additional cost of materials or making time. Alternatively by spending even more time on a piece to increase its quality or complexity you may be able to sell in a better market.

INCREASE THE PERCENTAGE OF TIME SPENT MAKING. Perhaps you are not using your week efficiently and are spending too much time on other jobs. If you can increase the percentage of the week spent making, the cost of each object will be reduced.

LOOK AT YOUR PRODUCT. Perhaps other objects would be more saleable, for example ones that are quicker to produce and therefore cheaper to make but which can command a good price. Some craftspeople find that an easily and quickly made range of objects can provide a bread-and-butter income which helps subsidise their own creative work. An alternative might be to use the workshop to make some other type of work which you know will sell. For example, some potters produce jewellery. However, there is a danger of the other work taking over and leaving you too little time for what you really want to do. And whatever you make it is important that the quality remains high as it is excellence you are selling.

SUBSIDISE YOUR PRODUCTION BY EARNING MONEY IN OTHER WAYS.
Many craftsmen and women subsidise or complement the income from their craftwork by taking on part-time work. At best these are jobs which relate to your skills; part-time teaching or design work.

However it may even need to be some unrelated work which can pay the workshop bills while you are building your reputation and a market for your work.

Local museums, arts centres, libraries and tourist centres may be interested in craft demonstrations or lectures, but be careful to receive an adequate fee. Most Regional Arts Boards organise residencies in schools and community situations, which pay well and can lead to useful contacts.

In conclusion

In the end if you have tried everything you can and are still not selling you will have to decide whether you wish to continue to make that particular work. The reality may be that there is little or no market at any reasonable price for the work you are producing. Perhaps your innovative work is ahead of the market. If so you just have to hope that you are not a Van Gogh and so ahead of the market that you will be dead before any of the work sells!

If you do want to continue then the only way will be to subsidise your making. This approach – spending part of the time making work to be sold at less than its true value and the rest using one's skills in other ways to earn money to live – has a long tradition in the crafts. And if it enables you to continue to create work with which you are pleased it can be a realistic and appropriate approach.

Selling

If you are to survive it is crucial that you sell what you make. When considering starting up your own workshop, it is important that you have some idea of what you plan to make – the clearer, the better. Knowing what you are going to make will enable you to carry out some market research.

Researching the market

Given the individuality of craft objects it can be difficult to assess the demand for work until some actual selling is attempted. Before you start your business it is a good idea to produce a sample of what you plan to make to see the response. If you are still at college you can use the work you make there to test the market, although you must be careful that your prices accurately reflect the prices you would have to charge when paying for premises, etc. If you have not already made any work, then the best thing is to produce some, perhaps by borrowing facilities, so that you can get a response before committing yourself to renting a workshop and buying expensive equipment. An enthusiastic response will give you the confidence you need to make the big step into self employment. If there is no interest at all, then perhaps you should think again.

Whether you are starting out or are already in business, it is important that you identify the potential purchasers for your work and match your products to them. He/she is not necessarily the owner of the nearest craftshop. You should consider every possible market where someone could use or own the work you make. Look at what else is available; assessing the competition is an important part of market research. The fact that you can make what you design often gives you an edge over those who are merely designers. Your flexibility offers you the competitive advantage of being able to provide an individual answer to a specific need.

Whether your work consist of one-off items best suited to exhibitions, large items made to commission, or batch orders requiring several sales outlets, you will need to put aside both money and time to promote sales. The budget might include paying for good photographs to circulate to galleries, the cost of a stand and attendance at a trade fair, or a professionally produced brochure aimed at prospective commissioning clients. Markets differ greatly and time would be well spent on seeking out the best potential buyers and devising the most effective method of presentation. Discovering where best to direct your promotional efforts will save you time in the long term.

Never forget that it is the individuality of design and quality of making which attracts buyers to the crafts. Craft objects can seldom compete on price terms with factory-produced objects, so emphasise the individuality of your work by putting your mark – or, better still, your signature – on every object. This emphasis should be extended to any packaging, labelling or publicity material.

Selling from the workshop

It is true that some makers successfully sell all, or the bulk, of their work direct to people visiting their workshop, but you should consider this option with care.

The main advantage is that you can set the selling price yourself as no shop mark-up is involved. (If you also sell work through shops, note the point made on selling direct in the previous chapter). The other advantages are not having to deliver work to several outlets, and having direct contact with your customers which can provide useful feedback.

The major disadvantage is that you will have to deal with the people visiting your workshop and this can take up a lot of time and interrupt your making, which can make selling direct unprofitable. You will have to invest time and money in ensuring that prospective customers are attracted to the workshop, and provide a clean space for the work on sale. You will need to consult your local planning department if you are thinking of selling direct from your workshop.

Attracting prospective customers

Research shows that people are more inclined to spend money when they are on holiday, be it a week or a day trip, so tourists can be a valuable source of sales.

Visitors to your town or area are unlikely to know their way around so you should consider how best to help them find the workshop. Talk to your local tourist office to see if details of your workshop can be included in the information they distribute; if they can be convinced that your presence will help attract more tourists to the area, then you may even be able to get some financial help to build a viewing area or sales point. Some local councils are very good at sign posting, so investigate that possibility. If you decide on a poster, make sure that it is well designed and includes a simple map of where you are. Take care in siting the posters; hotels, if agreeable, are good sites, as are tourist offices and other tourist attractions. Check regularly to see that your posters are still there. Leaflets can also attract customers, although it is easy to waste money on them unless they are well directed. The Rural Development Commission or your local tourist office will be able to give advice on where best to place leaflets for maximum effect. Local newspapers are generally not so good for attracting tourists, but local radio can work fairly well.

Of course, visitors to the area will not be the only market for your work and you will also want to build up a reputation with those who live there. Word of mouth and personal recommendations count for a great deal and this needs to be encouraged by promotion. Local exhibitions, write-ups in the local press and national magazines, demonstrations at local fairs and shows all help.

When they arrive

You have to decide how to organise your space. If the workshop includes the sales area, it is best to separate the two in some way. Your display/sales area should show the work to the best advantage, and you should try to keep it and the work clean. How you present the work for sale will affect the price people will pay and their willingness to buy. High prices are unlikely to be paid if work is cluttered and dusty. Prices should be clearly marked on each piece. Information panels about the workshop, your work and yourself can save you having to answer the same questions time and time again, and details like "member of Crafts Council Selected Index" or "winner of such-and-such a prize" may encourage sales.

You will need packaging and it might be worth making this a feature. Specially printed boxes and bags, or work attractively packaged, can help sales. Many people are attracted by bargains so a "seconds" area is often a money-spinner.

If you are alone in the workshop, you will have to work out how to combine selling and making, with the minimum of disruption. People may come in to watch rather than buy and you will have to work out how best to turn visitors into customers. If a lot of people visit at once, then coping with both selling and making will become almost impossible and you may need to get help. Given the tax advantages of employing your spouse, paying your husband or wife to deal with sales may be an answer. If identifiable periods or days are particularly busy, then it may be best to limit employed help to those times. Some makers find it best to totally separate the shop area from the workshop, with visitors able to view work being made from a slight distance – a viewing area or through a window. This arrangement means that making can go ahead without interruption, while still encouraging sales, but it depends on having someone to look after the sales area all the time.

Selling by post

Postal selling is another method of selling direct. Placing advertisements in local newspapers is usually expensive, although this can encourage people to visit your workshop. However, if you have a particular product that you think might attract orders by post, then experiment with advertisements for this. If you wish to explore selling your work via national advertisements you must take account of the high cost, although if a small advertisement in a national Sunday newspaper or glossy magazine results in orders for six months the expense will have been justified.

Whether or not you should experiment with this method will depend on what you sell and on identifying the appropriate magazine or newspaper to advertise in. Selling by post will involve you in packing; see the next chapter for advice on how to avoid breakages.

For information on COD (cash on delivery) and other postal services, obtain a copy of the 'Royal Mail Inland Compendium', available free from Post Offices.

Selling through craft and trade fairs

For many makers the cost of table space at a local fair or market is the first expenditure on promotion. However, at all levels – from major international trade fairs to local craft markets – there are organisers eager to offer space. Fair organisation is an industry in its own right and, unless you know why you are taking part and are ready to take advantage of your investment, it is only the exhibition organiser who benefits. For every event ask yourself who will visit it and what they will be looking for. At the right event, you can meet a great number of customers for your work in a short time – probably more than by any other means – and you must be properly prepared to benefit.

Research

Your aim is to sell but much depends upon the nature of the event. You may be approaching a new market in which your work is unfamiliar, in which case the emphasis is upon presenting information and developing contacts to follow up later rather than making the bulk of your sales at the event. There are different sorts of events attracting different types of buyer, and approach and presentation must be tailored accordingly. Grand titles mean nothing and it is more important to check the number and type of visitor and records of previous sales than choose to show at the "43rd International Congress of the Multi-Dimensional Plastic Arts" just because of the title.

Do some research before committing yourself to a single fair by visiting a selection and learning from the mistakes of others: look at the stands, their layout, the leaflets available, the image presented and the way each stand is run. You will see busy stands enjoying obvious success and others where disconsolate people stand alone looking bored, or sit buried in a book, newspaper or their lunch. Why? It is not necessarily the quality of the work. Either the stand is wrongly designed, the staff are uninterested or they are at the wrong event – perhaps all three!

Apart from choosing the right event and the appropriate presentation, take note of the siting of your stand. If you are close to the main entrance visitors may take immediate notice or they may walk straight past, while stands near catering facilities may attract dirty glasses, plates and wrapping paper. If you cannot get a reasonable position you could ask for a reduction in the stand cost to offset the poor site.

PRE-PLANNING

If you decide to show then be prepared. Making a pile of everything you produce will not work – not even at a local exhibition. Choose items of your work which most closely meet the requirements of your potential customer. A busy buyer is unlikely to spare a second glance at a poorly presented group of work, and the more professional your display the more it will attract attention.

Budget for costs over and above the hire of the space. These will include display and furnishing fittings, publicity material and promotional costs, travel and subsistence. At larger events the organisers will provide a shell stand. This may be little more than walls possibly with a raised floor and/or a lightweight ceiling. There may be severe restrictions on painting, covering or fixing items to the walls, so your displays should probably be prefabricated and free-standing. You may want to consider additional lighting and floor covering (both are sometimes offered by the organisers but are often expensive). Good stand lighting should be an important element in your display.

Work out the area of the stand beforehand and test the assembly and display of everything. The more pre-planning of the display you can do, the more relaxed you will be when the show starts. These events are very tiring because you must continually take the initiative with visitors and potential customers.

AT THE EVENT

Make sure you are noticed among all the other exhibitors. Some makers demonstrate, particularly at smaller events. This should be done with caution. It is likely to be more effective where public relations rather than sales are the aim, because when you are demonstrating you cannot be selling or paying attention to potential customers passing the stand. An immediate process, such as raising a pot or wood turning, may draw a sufficient crowd to prevent buyers reaching you and can deter sales. Yet there is nothing more compelling than a television screen – an audio-visual display may serve you better than a demonstration. A slide presentation can illustrate your craft techniques and a short repeated video tape will act as another "salesman " by briefing passers-by about your work.

Having got potential customers to stop at your stand, there are two essentials: you may secure an order, but even if you do not, get the visitor's name and address (and possibly also what they do for a living so you can assess their purchasing potential) and have something they can take away by which to remember you and your work. You can meet potential customers at such events and you should always be ready to record their details. Contacts from these events are vital and can be followed up later. Equally you hope that the buyer will contact you. To help them you need some well-produced, promotional literature, preferably with an illustration. You can use this material elsewhere, of course, but it must be of a quality worth keeping. If the alternative is a pile of hand-written photocopied notes, then have nothing. Well-designed and simply printed leaflets do not need to be expensive. Resist the tendency to do everything as cheaply as possible. It will be noticed and reflect on your work. See page 166 for advice on producing promotional material.

To begin with you may make little impact at these events, and it may be better to put your effort into one large and particularly appropriate fair or exhibition rather than into several small ones. Your presence implies that you are sufficiently well organised to attend and take advantage of the event, and capable of producing the orders which you hope for. You will get a direct response, with an opportunity to learn about customers' views on the work and its place in the market you are seeking to develop. While the quality of your work will ultimately determine your success, some thought and careful planning will shorten the process and prevent time-consuming and expensive mistakes.

Selling to shops

First of all, look around to see which shops might be interested in selling your work. Specialist craft shops vary from the ultra-traditional to the ultra-contemporary and you need to judge which seem most suited to the type of work you are producing. The Crafts Council's Map list of selected shops, available free, may be useful in drawing your attention to possible outlets. Of course, craft shops are not the only places to consider as outlets for your work. Fashion boutiques might be interested in jewellery and scarves, toy shops in wooden objects, kitchen shops in bowls, etc. Also, while you are looking round for possible retail outlets for your work, it is worth seeing if there are gaps in the market which you might fill by producing a specific range of work.

Given that to survive you are going to have to sell most of what you make, you will either have to find a few outlets which can sell a lot of your work or many outlets which can each sell a few items. As selling involves visits and travelling (which cost money and mean less time making), the best answer is a limited number of retail outlets each selling a lot of work, but clearly your answer will depend on the response and your particular circumstances.

Approaching outlets

Initially, it is probably best to select a few shops to approach at a time. Then as your business expands you can develop more outlets. In the early stages you will need to allow quite a bit of time for visiting shops to show them your work, probably one day a week. Try and ensure that you have a good range of work at this point so that you have plenty to show.

You should spend time researching which outlets are likely to be appropriate for your particular work and then draw up a priority list. For instance, if there are three outlets in the same town all of which stock your type of work make sure you contact the most prestigious first. You can always try the second on your list if the first is not interested. Targeting a particular geographical area, such as South Wales, is one way to begin. This helps reduce travel expenses and time spent away from the workshop. Once you have fully covered one area you can move on to another.

Having decided which shops you are going to approach, write or telephone to arrange an appointment. Retailers are busy and do not like people calling in without some prior arrangement. In fact, without an appointment you will often be unable to see them. So arrange an appointment and make sure that you arrive on time. If appropriate, write a postcard or a brief note confirming the time, perhaps sending some publicity material about the work. Retailing practice varies in different areas and in some cases, such as fashion shops or department stores, you may find it extremely difficult to get appointments with buyers. Only experience will tell you the best way to approach these shops. If all attempts to obtain an appointment fail, it may be worth just arriving on the doorstep and asking to see the buyer. However, if you cannot, you need to decide quickly whether it is worth showing your work to someone else. You should find out whether you are dealing with someone who has the power to decide whether to buy or order your work. Showing work to sales assistants or subordinate members of staff can be counter-productive. If they like your work and recommend it to the owner, you have to come back and make another sales pitch. If they do not like it, they could wreck any opportunity to see the buyer at a later date by making unhelpful comments.

 Think about how to present your work. If you make small items, you might find it worthwhile to have a display case which will ensure that your work is always seen in the right conditions – jewellery heaped on a counter already covered in paperwork may not look as impressive as the same work displayed in a custom-built box. Think about how you present yourself. If you are visiting a smart shop in the hope of selling them expensive pieces, looking scruffy may have an adverse effect. If you make work that is designed to be worn, wear it yourself and that way the buyer can see how it looks on someone.

Before your visit, think about what you are going to show and what you are going to say. Take along enough of your work to give a clear indication of your range. Know what each piece costs; there is nothing worse than not being able to give a precise reply when asked for wholesale prices. You do not need to memorise your prices, consulting a neatly prepared price list is fine. Calculate beforehand how many pieces you can produce and in what time-span. If you are given an order, there is the danger that you will agree, in the heat of the moment, to providing far more than you can produce or in too short a time. State at the time what you can actually produce rather than phoning back the next day to say that you cannot in fact carry out what was agreed. Be confident and business-like. Presumably you believe in your work and think people will wish to buy it. Craft retailers will be more likely to buy from you if they can see a consistency and conviction in your work and yourself.

Taking orders

Always take a supply of order forms with you. If the shop orders work on the basis of what you have shown them, obtain a written order or write out one on their behalf, detailing the price, the number and the delivery date. If you write one on their behalf, give them one copy and retain the other.

It may be that for some reason you are uncertain about accepting a good order. Perhaps it may conflict with workshop schedules, other delivery dates, or need materials difficult to obtain. In such circumstances rather than take an order on which you might default you could make it "subject to confirmation". If so ensure this is written on to the order.

If you leave work on a sale-or-return basis ensure you write out a sale-or-return record with full descriptions and prices and ask the shop owner to sign your copy as confirmation of receipt.

If unsuccessful

If you receive an order or make a sale, you will be able to go to other shops with renewed confidence. But what if they say "No"? Do not accept their "no" without question. Most craftspeople are understandably nervous about selling their work, and the normal reaction to a rejection is to presume that the person hates the work and to run for the door. However, the reason for the "no" may have nothing to do with the quality of the work; if you do not ask, you will never know the reason. So ask "Why not?", a simple question which may elicit an answer that will allow you actually to make a sale. "I don't like the colour" could be the reason, and offering to supply an alternative colour could turn the "no" into a "yes." Similarly "I don't like that style" could lead to showing a different design and a sale. "I was really looking for teapots" could lead to a further meeting to which you could take those teapots you decided not to bring along the first time. It may be that they do not have the resources to purchase work at present but expect to start buying again in a month or so. Of course, it may be that the price is too high for their clientele. In such cases resist dropping your price.

Do not be put off revisiting a shop that has said "no". With certain places it may take several visits before your work is accepted. Going back to a shop proves to them that you are still in business and have commitment. If it is quite simply that they do not like your work, do not be discouraged. It is simply their view and others may have a better appreciation of your greatness! However, if you try several outlets which all turn your work down, it may be worth asking someone whose judgement you trust to give you their opinion on the work.

Providing work on sale-or-return

Many shops operate on the basis of "sale-or-return" which means that they will only pay for goods after they have been sold. This is an unfortunate practice as makers are in effect being asked to provide the capital finance to stock the shop, something that should clearly be the retailer's responsibility. It should be up to the shop to back their judgement by buying the work outright. However when you are starting out, it is hard to avoid the practice of sale-or-return, but you should consider whether or not it is worth accepting it in every case. If the shop promises to be a particularly profitable or prestigious outlet, you may well feel that to give them work on sale-or-return is reasonable as it will create a useful future trading contact. If you are trying to encourage retailers to take work which is clearly outside their normal stock, sale-or-return may convince them to stock it. In such cases suggest that they reduce their normal commission/mark-up and increase your wholesale price (so that the retail price remains the same) to compensate for them not buying the work outright.

If you do leave work on a sale-or-return basis, it is worth checking after a week or two that it is actually on display. There is little point in it being there if it is left in a box under the counter. Similarly, see that it is being well displayed. As the shop has not paid for the work, there is always the danger that they will not work so hard at selling it as work for which they have paid. Check at regular intervals to see if the work has been sold. If it has make sure to issue an invoice. If it is not selling, offer to exchange the work for other pieces as it is bad for you and the shop for the public to see a particular item on the shelves for too long. If your work does sell and the shop wishes to stock more, it may be worth trying to insist that they now buy at least some of it, perhaps providing additional work on sale-or-return so that a wider range can be displayed. It is very difficult to avoid the sale-or-return problem, but you should try to work towards outlets buying your work outright as their confidence in your selling power grows.

Remember that people who run craft shops generally do it for love rather than money. Most make very small profits and owners often subsidise their shops, either from other sources or by paying themselves little. Do not get the idea that craft shops are out to exploit you. The request that you leave your work on sale-or-return is a result of their own cash flow problems, and their mark-up is merely their charge to cover overheads, service, contacts and general marketing expertise.

Craft shops are always looking for interesting new work to sell and it is up to you, initially at least, to go out and make your work known to them.

Working to commission

The intention to make commissions a part of your business needs careful thought. Commissioned work can be more profitable than speculative work but it does not suit everyone and calls for a highly professional approach, for what is being sold initially is only an idea and the commissioner must have confidence in the maker's ability to translate it into something tangible. It is a very individual service and new business is often dependent upon personal recommendation and the maker's reputation. The decision to undertake commissions, therefore, contains three elements; being properly organised to promote and accept commissions, developing a reputation as someone who responds quickly, energetically and creatively, and having the determination to succeed in a specialised field.

In preparing for commissions, consider exactly what they entail for you and your methods of working. Securing an order, possibly in competition with other designers, means that you must be certain that you can discuss your work, designs, production and delivery dates with complete confidence. You will need a diary and a workshop schedule to assess quickly your ability to accept work within a fixed time-scale.

Clients must be able to contact you. You should consider whether to rent or buy a telephone answering machine. If you do not have a telephone of your own, find someone who will always take messages for you, or perhaps use one of the small office service agencies. Whatever method you use, make sure that people can contact you quickly and easily – commissions rely on this.

You must be certain of up-to-date prices for materials and their availability. Iron out early problems or the client may approve designs for which you cannot get the materials you have specified.

A letter may be your first contact with a client. Although neat handwriting is quite acceptable, typing is almost always easier to read. However, even if writing by hand, use carbon paper and keep a copy; it is impossible to remember what you have written to everyone. If you have a telephone conversation at which important points and/or changes are agreed then write down the points and write to the client stating the key points which were agreed in the phone call. If these were major changes you should ask them to write back confirming them. Or if the changes are small you might just write something like "Unless I hear from you within a week I will presume that you agree the points which we discussed and agreed when we spoke on the telephone on x date." (Then list the points).

Duplicate notebooks are useful; when you have mislaid your notes of a meeting, telephone conversation, order or any other information, you always have a back-up copy. Keep the notes and all correspondence (including copies of all your letters to the client) in a simple filing system.

Check lists are helpful to remind you at every stage of the things which are so easy to forget. They range from your needs for the first visit to a client (notebook, diary, photographs, samples, tape measure and client's address!) through to delivery of the work (essential assembly tools, duster, repair kit, notebook and tape measure in case of another commission).

First meeting

Of all the meetings that you have with a client, the first is probably the most important. It is then that you establish confidence in your work and your credibility as a maker. If you are visiting the client make sure that you are on time, with everything you need. If you are late, ill-equipped or unprepared you are at a disadvantage from the start.

Be clear where you have got to be – and how to get there! Have the client's telephone number handy and, if you are delayed, ring to say so.

If the client is coming to you, you should have somewhere clean and tidy to make your presentation. If the workshop does not have an area which you can keep for such meetings, you may be able to use a nearby hotel lobby or somewhere similar. But remember that pubs and other public places can be noisy and very distracting.

 Both you and the client will be assessing each other at this first meeting. Try and ensure that there are the fewest possible diversions to break your concentration. You will be less self-conscious if you dress to fit the occasion. A suit may be out of place if the client always wears T-shirts. It will be easier to build up a rapport with clients if you know something about them or perhaps their business, so a little research should pay dividends.

Probably you will know roughly what is wanted. Choose a small selection of photographs and/or drawings specifically for the occasion and again matched to the client. It is not necessary to run through your life's work, but a little variety with one or two unexpected designs might show something the client did not know you made and encourage additional work.

In discussing work never be afraid of saying "no." Should you be unhappy about working for the client, or feel for any reason that you cannot tackle the job, then do not go ahead. A bad commission could do you more harm than no commission. Refusing a commission may also mean taking the trouble to explain why. The personal nature of commissioning means that a careful explanation can result in the client varying the terms, possibly making the job acceptable. You could be asked to submit ideas for another commission at some future date because of the care with which you handled a refusal.

You must expect to assemble a detailed brief at the meeting. If you are visiting the client, try to ensure that you do not have to go back to take further measurements or ask for additional information. You should establish exactly what is wanted: dimensions, materials, colour and any specific limitations, as well as noting the style and taste of the client. You will need to know delivery dates and whether elements of the commission could be affected by other factors such as structural work or redecoration which need to be completed first.

You must establish quickly what the client is expecting to pay. Broaching the subject of money at an early stage is something many makers find difficult but it is essential. You can approach the subject by saying that the type of work being considered is usually in the range of £x to £y. While you want to avoid putting off a prospective client, it is sensible to quote at a higher rather than lower level as this leaves scope for negotiation. Unless you start discussing the likely price you may end up spending a lot of time talking over the idea only to find that the person is not really serious. If your work is simply not possible at the price, say so at once. Exciting designs may encourage an increase in the preliminary figure, but you must avoid any possible misunderstanding and be clear about the financial limitations.

You may well plan to attract work in the early days by keeping charges low but you must guard against working below your cost price. The one exception to this rule can be where you wish to carry out a large scale commission but without ever having done one you cannot prove to clients that you can! This Catch-22 may mean carrying out the first commission for a less than realistic price. Such a loss can, of course, be construed as a promotional expense. An opportune, well-executed commission which loses money may establish your credibility with a client and open the door to a great deal of highly profitable work. You must gauge the long-term benefits carefully and take the gamble if it seems right, but don't plan to do it too often and where you do, make it clear that you are carrying out the work at less than your normal rate and that any subsequent commissions will need to be at a higher price. You must guard against getting a reputation for being too cheap. It is a sure recipe for going out of business. A reputation for creativity and reliability is what you need.

It may be appropriate for you to make a separate design agreement at this stage. You might charge a standard fee, or a sum may be included in the main commission agreement. Whatever the case, you should agree with the client that you will be paid for your design work, whether it is accepted or not, and obtain payment of the design fee before commencing work. If the customer is serious about the commission they should accept paying the design fee, or a reasonable deposit, in advance.

The last point is to agree the date when you will present your designs. It will be an important moment and you will want to ensure you can get everything ready, so make certain the agreed date allows for existing commitments.

Preparing the design

While there is complete freedom to express yourself in the proposals you submit, it is fundamental that your designs must satisfy the client's brief. However well presented your ideas, the client is unlikely to proceed with the commission if you have not designed what he/she wants or needs. You can of course show additional designs and amendments in the hope of varying the brief if there is something appropriate you would particularly like to produce.

In discussing designs you may well have to protect clients from themselves. It is pointless slavishly agreeing with a client's wishes if you know that what is wanted will collapse under its own weight or draw blood every time it is worn ! If you cannot get an agreement about the essential practical elements for the work, do not go ahead with the work: again, a bad commission is probably worse than no commission.

In preparing your suggestions, be conscious of the longevity of the work, as well as the need for maintenance. Future commissions and the possibility of more work will suffer if you are constantly being asked to adjust, repair or service earlier pieces.

If you are making something large for a specific place, make sure that it can be got where it will be needed. You may have to alter your designs in order to get the work through a door if you cannot assemble it on site. Even for a small item this can be a limiting factor; your client, without mentioning it, may be expecting to keep something in a safe or cupboard with restricted access.

The greatest limitation on your design will be cost, and you must change your ideas if you cannot produce them within the proposed figures. You can always draw up properly costed amendments and additions showing how the designs could be improved.

Presenting your design

When you come to show your designs, make sure they are properly presented. It may be necessary to give the designs explanatory titles and reference numbers to avoid misunderstandings. Figures and dimensions should be noted on all the drawings, together with details of the materials to be used. If the client does not understand design drawings, you can either produce a small maquette or draw a sketch of the piece. It is always a good idea to produce samples of the materials to be used and the finishes which you have planned.

If you are submitting designs for a large commission, particularly where this is in competition with others, presentation of your idea can be crucial. If those selecting the design idea are unused to looking at drawings and plans, a model or photographs of the site with the design superimposed on may be appropriate.

 When clients approve the design you should consider asking them to note their acceptance on the appropriate drawing. If you have provided a selection from which to choose, the client's signature will prevent confusion later.

The approval of the design is a significant moment and may be the time for you and your client to sign the commission agreement. If appropriate, you can now submit the invoice for any balance of your design fee, and (on receipt of the agreed initial payment) begin production.

During production

When production is under way the client may wish to see the work in progress. You should decide whether or not you will make a practice of this. Many makers feel clients should not see the apparent chaos of a workshop, which can discourage them. For others, demonstration of the skills and processes of production are an essential element of involving the client in the creation of an individual piece.

If for some unavoidable reason you need to alter the specification, you must consult the client. If you vary the specifications without permission the client can legally refuse to pay.

Time schedules are important. If you have agreed a date for completion of the commission you will be in breach of your contract if you do not complete it by this date. This can result in the client refusing the work and even, in certain situations, asking for compensation. This is particularly relevant if you are working as part of a larger contract – on a new building, for example – where your failure to deliver on time could hold up other contractors. Even if no specific completion date has been agreed, you must supply the commissioned work within a reasonable period of time. The relevant legislation is the Supply of Goods and Services Act 1982.

If you do run into difficulties with a piece, always inform the client of any potential delay. It is never easy making excuses for being late, but it helps if you have given warning that it is likely to happen.

Whether production is on schedule or not, you should let your client know when it is nearly complete. Completion may involve the client in getting ready to receive the work or, perhaps more important, in making arrangements to have the money ready to pay you. In any case, advance warning at this stage should heighten anticipation of the eagerly awaited delivery.

Delivery

Having advised the client that the work is almost ready, arrange delivery only when it is complete. There can always be last-minute snags for both you or your client. The details of responsibility and costs for this stage should have been agreed long ago, but you should plan the delivery or installation in detail.

Make sure that you have test-assembled everything and that you have sufficient people to help you. Your reputation could be severely dented if you turn up expecting your client's family to manhandle heavy items into a confined space. You must have the necessary tools for assembly with you, as well as a kit to repair or retouch any minor damage on the spot. Be prepared to take advantage of the success of the commission to develop another, possibly having thought about a companion piece, and be equipped to take notes and measurements as necessary.

 If the work is to be installed by someone else, as part of a larger building contract for example, you will need to judge whether it would be sensible for you to be there in case of problems.

It is important to recognise that the delivery or installation of the commission is a crucial moment for your client. For you this may be just more work, but for the client it may be the first time they have ever commissioned a craft work. It may be that with a little imagination or some extra expenditure you can make the first sight, or unveiling, win an additional advantage. The pleasure of experiencing the new commission can be ruined if it is badly presented, and for your client the climax of the process should be taking possession of the work. Given that it is common for those who have successfully commissioned work from craftspeople to commission further pieces, ensuring that you do everything to make the experience of the commission successful is important.

Payment

As has already been stated, do not be reticent about discussing money – you cannot survive without it. If you have discussed payment from the outset and both parties are clear about the costs involved, there should be no confusion. The commission agreement should state when payments are due. It is then up to you to submit your invoices at the appropriate stages. You cannot expect the client to pay without them.

Because of the particular nature of commissions, you should guard against proceeding with work at any stage if payment is over-due or you have reason to believe it could be withheld. If you keep going without receiving the agreed payments, you may find that your reward is possession of something which is totally unsaleable to anyone other than your defaulting client.

Unless you have breached the contract, the client is legally bound to pay for the finished work, or all the work done to that date. The fact that they decide they do not like the finished piece is not sufficient grounds for refusal to accept it and pay in full if you have worked to the agreed design.

Learning to talk about money with confidence and making sure that you do not carry out more work than necessary without payment are important factors in commissions. You cannot develop a business without taking some risks, but you can keep them to a minimum.

The commissioning contract

Central to the commissioning process is the contract with the client. The contract is an agreement for you to supply skill, materials and labour in producing an object in return for a sum of money. In its simplest form it is a verbal request by the client (commissioner) for the work to be undertaken, but it is far more satisfactory if the agreement is in writing. With a simple straightforward commission, the least which should be accepted is an exchange of letters. Disputes about payment, quality, damage and a whole range of other factors may occur, and the contract protects both parties. You may find it useful to develop a standard contract, perhaps containing clauses specifically relevant to your work and if you are carrying out commissions regularly you could ask a solicitor to draw up a standard contract. AN PUBLICATIONS have produced a useful factsheet on this subject.

Given the variety of commissions it is difficult to give a simple example of a contract. The following are all points which need to be considered.

THE PARTIES TO THE AGREEMENT

State who the agreement is between, particularly if the commissioner is a company or organisation rather than an individual. If you are being commissioned by an architect on a building project, you may be asked to work as a sub-contractor to the main building contractor, and it is likely that such a contract will contain penalty clauses which can be severe if delays occur in delivering the commissioned work. It is advisable to try and steer clear of such a contract and instead ask to be contracted directly by the architect.

WHAT WILL BE MADE

A full description of what it has been agreed you will produce, including any design specifications, e.g. dimensions. The description may also carry reference numbers to the appropriate design drawings.

MATERIALS

Detail the materials to be used where important, with exact descriptions, such as the fineness of precious metals, if necessary. The use of scarce, unusual or exotic materials may involve unforeseen expenditure, particularly if the job is a long one. You should consider a clause making clear the basis on which such materials will be charged. This might be at cost or as a supplement should their cost rise above an agreed figure.

DESIGN FEE

A commission for which a new or reworked design is required should include a clause agreeing a fee for the design work. This fee should be payable whether or not the client goes ahead with the commission. Depending upon the nature of your work, you may have a standard fee.

THE FEE PAYABLE AND PAYMENT STAGES

The full cost and details of payment stages. Misunderstandings can occur if the number, method and timing of payments are not agreed and so these must be stated. It is usual for payment to be made in three or four parts, the first when the commission is agreed, part when it is half completed and the final payment on completion and delivery. Where special or expensive materials are involved or the commission is expensive, a larger number of part-payments may be required. If appropriate, stipulate the method of payment. It may be necessary to state in which currency the agreed fees will be paid, particularly if dealing with an overseas client. There will be less risk if the payment is made in sterling.

Completion date

The date by which the commission is to be completed or, if no specific date, the time limit for the project. If you have agreed a date for completion of the commission you will be in breach of your contract if you do not complete it by this date. This can result in the client refusing to pay for the work and even, in certain situations, asking for compensation. This is particularly relevant if you are working as part of a larger contract – on a new building, for example – where your failure to deliver on time could hold up other contractors. Even if no specific completion date has been agreed, you must supply the commissioned work within a reasonable period of time. The relevant legislation is the Supply of Goods and Services Act 1982.

Change of ownership

It is usual to stipulate that the work remains the maker's property until receipt of final payment. The question of ownership could be important if there are problems over payment, particularly if the work might be delivered before the final payment has been received.

Amendments

After accepting your design and work has begun, the client may wish to vary the terms of the commission. You should state the basis on which alterations will be charged. This would normally be your hourly rate for making the changes and any additional material costs. You must consider whether and how to charge for work already completed which has to be abandoned due to alterations.

Cancellations

Cancellation is always a bad moment and, while it may be due to circumstances over which your client has no control, if a contract has been signed then the client will be legally bound to reimburse you for all costs incurred up to the point of cancellation. However, given the difficulty of agreeing what should be paid, a cancellation clause should be seriously considered as an essential part of any commission agreement and should outline the basis on which the calculation for your own charges will be made. A fee calculated on the number of hours worked is the simplest and most easily agreed method, although it may be necessary to relate the figure to the proportion of the commission completed at cancellation.

Arbitration

This clause need only stipulate that in the event of a dispute an independent arbitrator will be agreed, or it may name the arbitrator.

Delivery and installation

Special arrangements may be necessary to deliver or install the work. It should be clear who will pay for any additional costs involved in delivery and who is responsible for and who will pay the costs of installation. If there are additional costs related to installation this needs to be made clear. Should a third party be involved in shipping or delivering the work, consideration must be given to the need for insurance and a clear statement made regarding responsibility for loss or damage during this phase.

Defects

The maker has an obligation to supply goods of merchantable quality under the Sale of Goods act. However, the work may have minor imperfections and it is reasonable to specify a period, say seven days following delivery, during which any defects should be reported which would be repaired at your expense. Such a clause would guard against claims for damage caused subsequently. It is worth noting, however, that the maker remains liable for hidden defects.

Copyright

Even where a work is commissioned the copyright in the work remains the maker's. However when commissioning work many clients will assume that copyright will pass to them with the work so you should make it clear that this is not the case. If they wish to own the copyright and you are agreeable, a clause transferring the copyright to them needs to be included.

Chargeable extras

You may wish to charge for incidental extras, such as travel expenses, over and above the fee. What is to be charged should be agreed in advance and clearly stipulated.

Developing commissions

If commissioned work is to be developed as a significant proportion of your production, a specialised promotional approach will probably be necessary. It takes considerable time to build up a reputation to the point where commissions are self-generating. In addition to being organised to take commissions, you must also be able to make a specific appeal to the clients who are likely to commission you.

It may be appropriate to produce simple, concise and well-illustrated promotional material. This should show the range of your work and the type of commissions which you undertake, as well as implying your competence and ability to work to commission. Such material can be used in a variety of ways to place your name and services before potential clients.

Some types of work may be sufficiently straightforward for promotional material and the commissioning agreement to be combined as an illustrated order form. Should this be the case, it is important that clients have space and suitable guidance to set out their instructions very clearly. However, this will only be appropriate for more repetitive work where the terms and conditions are standard.

If you have promotional material you will need to plan carefully how best to circulate it. There are many professional organisations, architects, interior designers, the advertising industry and others, through whom you might contact those most likely to be interested in what you make. There are a number of agencies involved in developing the commissioning of art and craft in public places and you should contact these with details of your work. Details of these are contained in the final chapter. The Crafts Council has a national register open to all makers and a Selected Index to which you can apply. Most Regional Arts Boards also have indexes of slides of regional makers and you should contact the relevant regional arts board to find out about such a service. Most operate slide indexes and for those which are relevant to your work, you should make every effort to meet the criteria for selection in order to take advantage of the additional publicity.

To gauge more immediately reactions to the service you offer, you could assemble a carefully chosen selection of names from the appropriate categories of a professional or local directory such as Yellow Pages and send them the information. By following this up with a telephone call and perhaps a visit, you will get a direct response and be able to judge which sections of the market are or are not likely to be worth pursuing. Remember the personal nature of commissioning. When contacting organisations, groups or companies, always try and identify the appropriate individual and write to them by name and not just by title or job description.

It should now be apparent why the professionalism of your promotional material is essential. If your first approach is through the letterbox, you must send something which is both interesting and worth retaining. Hand-written photocopies are worthless, yet people still try and use them.

As your reputation grows, your fee for working to commission can be expected to rise.

There are an increasing number of competitions for commissions. With some it is expected that submissions will be on a purely speculative basis with no design fees payable. It is important therefore when considering entry to a competition that you are quite certain of the terms under which it is being held. When no design fee is payable, you must estimate the cost to your business if your designs are not selected. Competitions can be worth entering, but they require extra effort if your work is to have a chance of selection. With this in mind you must consider not only the loss in unpaid design time if you are not successful, but also whether the competition is worth winning.

It may be that the nature of your work would allow a shop, gallery or other agent to attract business and undertake some of the negotiating on your behalf. You are probably a better designer and maker than promoter, and you should be aware of the benefits of getting others to help you attract work. Much will, of course, depend upon identifying appropriate shops or galleries who are sympathetic to your work and prepared to make a positive effort to encourage and promote a commissioning service.

As with other forms of retailing, it is perfectly reasonable for the agent or retailer to take a commission for promoting and selling your work. The amount will depend upon what they do. With your agreement, some may undertake initial negotiations, handling all the financial arrangements and dealings with the client, for which a fee of not less than 25% of the total commissioned figure is perfectly reasonable. Similarly, expect to pay an introductory fee of around 10% to any agent bringing business to you – even if you undertake all the dealings with the client yourself. Remember that this is work you would not have without someone else's efforts and be ready to include such fees in your estimates, regarding them as the cost of increased business, not reduced profits.

A more difficult problem is that of repeat fees should you be approached directly by a client who originally came to you via a gallery or agent, for a further commission. If an agent is actively promoting your work, he or she may well have played a part in the repeat order coming about. You should perhaps consider an arrangement whereby the agent receives a fee (say 5%) of any repeat business from a client within one or two years of the original commission. Again, it is a reasonable reward for finding you a good client. Whatever procedures you adopt, you should always find some way of repaying those who promote your work and introduce business to you – your next commission might depend on it.

As your promotional efforts begin to bring in work, remember to keep a proper record of successful commissions. It is worth investing in good photographs, particularly when you are pleased with the results of a commission. You can take your own photographs but they must be good. Bad photographs do you and the work no credit and should never be used. Promotional material can be greatly improved if you are able to include a well-illustrated case history which demonstrates clearly your ability to deliver the finished article.

The story of an interesting commission together with good photographs may attract magazine coverage. All such articles help build a reputation and offer a chance for further promotion. It may be worth paying for a run-on of the pages illustrating your work to send out with your promotional material to prospective clients. The more important the magazine, the more its reputation will assist you.

You should also be aware of the value of secondary publicity. You may have used specialist materials, tools or techniques. Always inform trade and technical journals who may be interested in some aspect of a commission. Perhaps your work used an unusual timber; photographs and details of the work sent to the marketing director of the timber importers, or even the commercial attaché at the embassy of the timber's country, may well give you substantial additional publicity if they highlight your commission for their own promotional purposes. Similarly, the work may have been produced using new tools, techniques or specialist skills which will be of interest to a far wider range of people than you would consider. Examine every opportunity where publicity, however obscure, can put details of your work before a new audience.

In circulating publicity and seeking promotion, obtain the permission of the client. Do not forget that the nature of commissioning may have given you access to confidential information. Quite apart from the question of copyright, which you must consider, you should get the client's agreement before you circulate details of his/her property. Your photographs could inadvertently show the siting of the office safe or the burglar alarm system!

 Provided that your clients are agreeable, it does no harm to circulate details of recent commissions at regular intervals to your personal mailing list. Repeat business is important and this information shows your newer work to those who have commissioned you before and demonstrates the demand for your services. They will probably enjoy hearing of your continued and growing success, which after all flatters their judgement in commissioning you in the first place, and may lead to them placing a further order.

Commissions come in all shapes and sizes. They can range from a small job for an individual to major pieces of work for large companies and local authorities. The scale of your response will depend upon the nature of the work. What is always important is the speed with which you respond and the professionalism of your approach. Commissions, more often than not, are won or lost on the enthusiasm and professionalism of your initial reply. In building your reputation and business, remember that it is your ability to react quickly that offers you a major advantage over and above your creative skills. You must be ready and willing to take that advantage.

Legal points

CONTRACTS

A contract, or binding legal agreement, may be verbal or written. With very few exceptions, a verbal contract is as binding as a written one. However, the problems arise when it is necessary to prove what was agreed verbally and this is why it is advisable that all business contracts should be in writing.

The most obvious contracts which craftsmen or women make are contracts for the purchase of materials and services from suppliers, or contracts for the sale of finished objects or services to shops and galleries or to members of the public. These contracts can be verbal but are better in writing. They can be a contract document or a letter, but should cover a number of standard points: the names of the buyer and seller, the items bought and sold, the price, the delivery date, place of delivery and any discount arrangements. There may be other points which should be written down to prevent disagreements later. The parties to the agreement will also be bound by a number of statutory requirements designed mainly to protect the consumer.

AN PUBLICATIONS have produced a series of useful contracts for artists and craftspeople as part of their Factsheets series. These are valuable guides and can be used as templates for your own contracts.

SALE OF GOODS ACT 1979

This act lays a number of obligations on both buyer and seller which come into operation in any contract for the sale of goods when the buyer and seller have not made a definite agreement on the various points. Some of the main obligations for a seller are: (a) That the goods sold are of " merchantable quality", i.e. are capable of doing what a buyer might reasonably expect them to do: a chair which collapses when sat upon would fail this test. (b) The goods must be fit for any particular purpose made known to the seller. Thus, if a buyer asks "Can this garment be machine washed?", the seller will be held responsible for the reply. (c) The goods must correspond with the seller's description of them, for example, a jug described as "a 3 pint jug" must hold 3 pints. (d) If the buyer has not examined the goods before delivery, he/she must be given a reasonable opportunity to do so. If the goods fail any of the tests above, the buyer is entitled to reject them, and be refunded in full.

SUPPLY OF GOODS AND SERVICES ACT 1982

This act extends many of the conditions set out in the Sale of Goods Act to contracts for the supply of services. Thus, in the absence of any express agreement between the parties, the following conditions apply: the work will be carried out with reasonable care and skill within a reasonable time, and the customer will pay a reasonable charge.
Although the act is useful, it is naturally much more business-like to establish both parameters of time and charges before the job commences.

TRADE DESCRIPTIONS ACTS 1968-1972

Under these it is also a criminal offence deliberately to misdescribe your goods whether verbally or in writing, including advertisements. A trade description covers such things as quality, method of manufacture, composition, fitness for the purpose, and the person who made it.

UNFAIR CONTRACT TERMS ACT 1977

This act was passed to prevent traders or suppliers slipping unfair exclusion clauses into contracts, typically in small print on the back of an invoice. Such clauses as "the maker accepts no responsibility whatsoever for any defects" no longer have much force, for it is up to the seller to prove that the exclusion clause is fair and reasonable in the circumstance.

CONSUMER PROTECTION ACT 1961

This act makes it an offence to sell or hold in stock any items which are covered by a series of regulations made under the act which are designed to protect the consumer from death or injury. Of particular relevance to craftspeople are the regulations for toys, glazed ceramic ware (if designed for use with food or drink) and domestic electrical equipment.
The penalties for non-compliance are severe, so makers should ensure that they have carried out the tests required by the regulations.

In addition, and this applies to any manufactured item, if a consumer or user comes to any harm as a direct result of the negligence of the maker, or even of the designer, he/she can sue for damages.

Hallmarking Act 1973

Hallmarking was introduced in 1273 and today it still ensures that a purchaser of a gold, silver or platinum item will not be defrauded. Every jeweller making work for sale must ensure that it is properly marked. The other side of the case, however, which causes a good deal of trouble for experimental jewellers is that an object, for example, made of gold with a small addition of decorative iron must not be hallmarked as gold. Indeed it is against the law even to describe it as gold and such a piece would have to be labelled "yellow metal and iron".

Sale-or-return or Consignment

This special type of sales contract is so common in the crafts world that it is worth noting the particular legal characteristics. Here, although the goods have passed from the maker into the possession of the shop/gallery, the ownership of the goods remains with the maker. In effect the shop/gallery is acting as an agent for the maker. As a consequence, the maker can take back the goods at any time and any risk to the goods (in the absence of negligence by the shop) also remains the responsibility of the maker, unless the shop accepts responsibility while the work is their possession. It also follows that when a sale to a member of the public finally takes place, the sale is technically between the maker and the ultimate buyer. The shop/gallery will have acted as agent for the sale and will charge the maker a commission for its services; VAT will be chargeable only on this commission. Because of these peculiarities, as well as the purely practical difficulties of keeping track of items out on sale-or-return, it is essential to maintain proper paperwork and to incorporate into the contract of sale-or-return with the gallery the clauses set out in detail on page 53.

140 Debt collection

Craftspeople who in general supply in small quantities are in an extremely vulnerable position when it comes to collecting their debts. If goods have been supplied on sale-or-return, it may take the maker many weeks of pestering and perhaps a visit to discover that a piece of work has been sold by the shop and that he/she is therefore owed the price less the commission. And then (and this applies to outright sales as well) if the retailer fails to pay, the maker will have to decide whether to take legal action over a small sum of money. For a sum of say, £50 it is hardly worth the legal fees, anxiety and sheer loss of making time. There is no answer to a most unfair situation once it has got to this stage. The real answer lies in being confident of the honesty of the retailer. Ask colleagues who already supply the outlet what their experience has been – does the retailer look after the work, pass back information on sales regularly and pay bills promptly.

If it does come to a court action it is now possible to take action yourself in the County Court for any amount of debt. This is a fairly easy process – contact the officials at your local County Court for information. You can take action for debts of less than £1,000 (1994/95 level) by 'informal arbitration'. A brief summary of the process was contained in the Crafts Council's newsletter 'Maker's News' Issue 5 (Autumn 1993) and a copy of this can be looked at in the Council's Library. Also a very useful detailed explanation of the process, explaining how to go about it, is set out in Croner's Reference Book For Self Employed which you should be able to consult at a reference library or the Crafts Council's library.

Before starting your legal action advise the person who owes you the money (the creditor) that you intend to take legal action. This may in itself bring a cheque.

Copyright

The Copyright, Designs and Patents Act 1988 includes works of "artistic craftsmanship" but for craft objects to qualify for inclusion they must have a discernible artistic quality rather than being merely utilitarian. However a utilitarian object would have design right protection if someone copied it for commercial purposes.

Copyright arises automatically with the creation of the work and no formalities or registration is required. It is wise however to add to every object and drawing the international copyright symbol ©, your signature and the date.

Under the above act the copyright in a work of "artistic craftsmanship" belongs to the maker ('the author' of the work) and the maker will remain the owner of the copyright for their life and for 50 years following their death unless he/she signs away the copyright to someone else. While craftspeople working in a freelance capacity own the copyright in something they create, if they are employed by someone else then the copyright in any object made as part of their employment would belong to the employer unless the contract of employment stated otherwise. Thus, for example, a craftsperson who sold a table would retain copyright in the table unless they signed over copyright to another. However a potter employed by a ceramics workshop would not have copyright in a teapot produced while working for the employer.

It should be noted that even where a work is specifically commissioned, copyright remains with the maker; again unless the maker specifically transfers copyright in writing.

 It has to be said that while craftspeople are often concerned that their ideas and designs will be copied by others, there are relatively few examples in the crafts of design ideas being 'stolen' in a way that is a provable breach of copyright. While it is illegal for anyone to copy another person's design or object, even quite small alterations to the original design can remove copyright protection. However, if you do come across a situation where you think someone is copying your work then you should investigate to see if they are breaking the law. If they are you may be able to sue them for damages.

A major revision to the law of copyright was the inclusion of moral rights for makers of original works of craft. This gives makers the right to insist on being identified as the maker whenever their work is exhibited in public, televised, included in a film or published commercially. It also gives them the right to object to derogatory treatment, which means if their work is subject to any addition, deletion, alteration or adaptation.

It is important to note than where your work is photographed by a photographer, whether or not commissioned by you, then they will own the copyright in the photograph(s), unless they transfer the copyright in the photograph(s) to you. Hence two copyrights exist. The second does not take precedence – the two copyrights exist alongside each other.

For further information on copyright and for a form of words to ensure that work is identified consult "Visual Arts & Crafts Guide to the New Laws of Copyright & Moral Rights" by Henry Lydiate, published by Art Monthly/Artlaw or "Copyright", by Roland Miller in the artists handbook series published by Artic Producers. The latter book also covers licences, designs, patents and trade marks.

The Design & Artists Copyright Society, Parchment House, 13 Northburgh Street, London EC1V 0AH (0171 336 8811) is a non-profit making organisation formed by artists to administer and protect copyright. DACS ensures that fees are paid to its members for reproduction of their work.

Registered Designs

If one of your designs is likely to be used for industrial production then you may wish to consider investigating registering the design. This is done through the Patents Office.

Trade marks

A trade mark is a symbol, which might be a signature, logo, monogram or words, by which goods are identified as being made or supplied by you.

They can be registered at the Register of Trade Marks but it seems unlikely that many craftspeople will find this fairly expensive process useful. In any case, if other people try to pass off their objects as yours, you could probably sue them under Common Law.

Exporting

 It is important to make a distinction between exporting as a business, compared to the technicalities of sending work abroad on one or two occasions. If you are determined to develop markets for your work overseas, then exporting should be a specific and planned element of your business for which you have clear and justifiable reasons. It will require time and money as well as a considerable amount of research and preparation. Without these, your efforts at exporting are likely to be buried beneath a mountain of paperwork or cripple you with unexpected costs.

If a friend returning from holiday comments "I saw one just like yours selling for five times the price", this is not a general signal to load the car and head for the nearest ferry. Nor are knowledge that someone else's work has sold well abroad or an inability to sell your work at home good reasons for believing you should be exporting. Selling abroad is likely to be more difficult than selling at home. However, you may be offered the opportunity of an exhibition abroad or an overseas buyer may show interest in your work and ask you to send some examples or place an order. You may be going on holiday and feel that it would be a useful opportunity to see whether there is any interest in what you make. In each case, you need to solve the practical difficulties of getting work abroad. It is important to recognise that as a single operation the time and costs involved may well make it unprofitable, although there are of course many other compensations, not least the satisfaction of having one's work exhibited or sold in other countries.

Before dealing with the practical problems of shipping ("shipping" is the general term used to describe transporting work abroad by any means) craft work, it would be useful to consider some aspects of the more formal development of exporting as part of your business. The first essential principle is to concentrate your effort. Certainly, it would be very nice to have your work spread throughout five continents but even the giant multi-nationals have enough difficulty achieving this. You are seeking to develop a market in a different culture with a different language; probably in a different time zone, with sizes in metric units and where the value of money changes every day in relation to the pound, quite apart from differing from country to country. Under these circumstances, even the European Union as one part of Europe is too diverse an area for you to tackle all at once. You would be best advised to pick a single country, or even a region within that country, where you have reason to believe that your work will attract a response and, having researched further, concentrate all your efforts on making a success of that market. If success comes, then growth and a further spread of your work will follow naturally.

Research

The formal channels for developing marketing research for exports are often inappropriate for the individual craftsperson. Naturally they tend to relate to clearly established product categories, and being told that a certain percentage of a country's gross national product is spent on giftware is of little value to you. The crafts seldom feature in such statistics and if they do it is often as a subdivision of a general giftware heading. But you are not looking for market research information about interest and opportunities in a general crafts market; you need to know whether there is specific interest in what you make and this is best obtained from those selling, or perhaps even making, similar pieces in the country in which you are interested.

For individual pieces of work, arts magazines, the magazines and newsletters of national craft organisations, specialist guild and society newsletters throughout the world all have advertisements, exhibition reviews and other editorial material in which details and addresses of specialised shops and galleries are given. Illustrations in gallery advertisements are a useful indicator of the style of work which is of interest to them.

The Department of Trade & Industry (DTI) in London, or through their regional offices, has information regarding commercial attachés, trade development officers and other staff abroad. The British Council should be able to provide details of their officers or embassy cultural attachés for the country in which you are interested. Rather than approach the organisations in this country, which will only carry more general information, you can then write abroad with specific and detailed enquiries. It is pointless asking the British Council or any similar organisation for general information, such as a list of galleries throughout Europe and America, but if you ask for details of galleries in Munich or a list of craft fairs in New York State, it is more likely that you will get a useful reply. The more specialised your questions the easier it is for them to be answered or for you to be given details of someone who can help you with information.

Your research may need to include other factors. Remember that goods imported into other countries often require specific marking or labelling, so it may be necessary for you to have wording such as "Made in England" on every piece. You will also have to consider whether your work could be affected by product liability conditions or legally imposed safety standards. This would particularly apply to toys and electrical goods, or in the United States to the lead and cadmium content in ceramic glazes. Extra shipping documents may be required. Some goods such as cheap, mass-produced textiles which have special duty or import restrictions can affect similar categories of work. Most countries therefore require a certificate showing the country of manufacture for textiles of any type, even a single wallhanging. Such certificates of origin are issued by the Chambers of Commerce. The DTI can usually advise on product specifications, legal and marking requirements, and the British Standards Institution (BTI) should be able to help with technical specifications, certainly within the European Union.

You can do a lot of research and indeed make sales to overseas buyers without leaving this country. Many of the larger overseas department stores and chains of shops have buying agencies here, usually in London. Many are looking for individual or small scale production work and approaching them can be an excellent way of testing foreign interest in your work. If you are successful, it is usual for them to undertake all the shipping and necessary documentation, paying you in sterling as soon as you fulfil their order as if selling in this country. The buying houses usually act for countries which are further afield, as European buyers can visit this country more easily. The Export Buying Offices Association can give details of the agencies for the country in which you are interested. A point to remember is that the buying houses themselves do not usually make the decision to purchase. They collect information, samples and all appropriate details about the work so that all the background research is done before store buyers come to this country on their purchasing trips. Although they are not the decision makers, they are usually well briefed in the likes and dislikes of the stores for which they act, the types of market served and the sales potential of the work that they see. So even if you are not successful in selling to them, you may get useful background information as to the likely appeal of your work in the country you are trying to tackle.

Major UK trade events, such as the Birmingham Spring Fair or 'Top Drawer', and certain craft fairs attract buyers from abroad and attending one of these may be a simpler first step in assessing the demand for your work both at home and among overseas buyers.

Pricing and costing terms

Before sending any work abroad, you must first consider how you are going to be paid. If pieces are going to an exhibition or on sale-or-return, make quite certain you know, and have agreed, the prices at which the work will be offered before it is sent. Preferably the agreement should be in writing, but if this is not possible before the shop or gallery has seen the work you must at least be clear about the rates at which commission or mark-up will be applied and who will organise and pay for the return of the unsold work. You should have agreed how the shipping costs will be met and the method of payment. Do not let your enthusiasm at being offered an overseas exhibition make you forget basic business practices. Once your work has left this country, you could have considerable difficulty in getting it either paid for or returned. You can ask for a banker's reference in advance, and for a single operation make ad hoc arrangements between your respective banks regarding the transfer of funds, using an International Money Order or by banker's draft, without having to resort to the more formal method of documentary credits. However, if you are looking to develop exporting in any serious way then export financing must be thoroughly investigated.

You will need to be familiar with some of the ways of quoting costs to overseas buyers. Unless they are visiting you in this country and making payment in sterling, they will probably want you to estimate the "landed costs". These represent the cost of your work plus customs duties and taxes, and specific elements of the shipping costs, usually up to arrival in the foreign country. You would be unwise ever to quote prices which include final delivery to a purchaser abroad unless you are using one of the delivery services, such as UPS who will invoice you in sterling, since these would also include local transportation costs as well as any customs duties and taxes which have to be paid. It is best to quote (possibly in foreign currency) in one of the following ways:

1. Ex-works. This is the basic cost of your pieces as if someone were collecting them from your workshop. 2. FOB (free on board). This is a comprehensive costing, including your ex-work price plus packaging and the cost of getting the shipment to an agreed port or airport of departure and loaded on the ship or aircraft. You would therefore quote "FOB Harwich"or "FOB Gatwick". 3. C & F (cost and freight). This costing details the price of the work and its carriage to the agreed point of arrival, which can be a port or an inland airport, for example "C & F Chicago". 4. CIF (cost, insurance and freight). This is the same as C & F with the addition of insurance costs for the consignment. Taxes and customs duties vary from country to country.

Within the European Union no custom duties are payable. No documentation is required other than the type of invoice you would send to a buyer in Britain in the normal course of your business. VAT is payable in all countries in the European Union and at different rates. Unless you are registered for VAT in the UK this will not affect you but you should be aware of the local rate as it can make a substantial difference to the retail price a shop or gallery must charge its customers. If you are registered for VAT you account for it on sales to other EU countries in the same way as you do in the UK. Now that the 'Common Market' has become the 'Single Market' it is as easy to transport work to Cologne or Copenhagen as it is to Cheltenham – the documentation and invoicing are the same.

Bearing in mind the constant change of rates of exchange, unless you have made careful calculations you would be well advised initially to quote prices in sterling. However when doing business or attending trade events in other countries it is important to have prepared detailed prices in the local currency. It is unlikely that you will be operating on a scale to take part in any of the export credit funding arrangements, but formal quotes and orders are important. A written order confirming a proposed purchase by an overseas buyer could be very useful in discussing finance with your bank manager! If you have taken the trouble to get the initial stages correct, you are likely to find other people much more helpful in solving the practical problems of getting your work shipped abroad.

Finally, if you seriously want to develop an export market, your work, its price, the way you distribute and sell it, and your promotional effort should from the outset be designed for and compatible with your buyer's market conditions rather than the pattern at home. Exporting may seem nothing but a mass of problems but many overseas markets are larger or more profitable than ours, and once you have made your first attempt the contacts and experience gained will make subsequent efforts easier.

How to do it

Customs and shipping procedures operate to a series of internationally agreed rules and the more you conform to standard procedures, the easier life will be. It is essential that you leave yourself sufficient time to find out what procedures are necessary before you arrive at a critical deadline – do not arrive at an international border with the boot of a car filled with individual objects which you claim to be valuable works of art or you are liable to complicate your life beyond your worst nightmares.

A major problem is that no international procedures recognise that all-embracing word "crafts". It depends upon the country involved whether work can be categorised as "works of art" and whether such a category is free of duty. The category is carefully defined and covers paintings, drawings and sculpture so that subjective judgements are avoided. Customs officers have to operate the rules and you cannot expect them to be altered for you. Descriptions of products are covered by an internationally accepted standard code and from this code you can establish what duty is payable. Know the code for your work and you can find the duty it will attract anywhere in the world. Defining your work correctly, and using the correct tariff code for it, is more than half the battle. If you appear unprepared or unhelpful, or expect customs officers to make artistic judgements about your work, you will run into problems. They are used to dealing with businesses familiar with customs procedures, whose documents have been carefully prepared in advance. Quantity and value are usually significant, so check what is allowed duty free. You can take some objects abroad as samples or within your personal gift allowance but don't expect to get away with six full tea chests. You might be allowed a single piece of furniture simply as a household effect but have difficulty taking a single piece of very expensive jewellery. Use your common sense but do not expect any sympathy if you deliberately set out to ignore or break the law.

Packing work

You must ensure work is properly packed. More money is lost through bad packing than almost any other cause and it is advisable to buy proper packing materials, and then include their price in your export costings. Look in Yellow Pages for packaging suppliers. Don't be tempted to cut corners; you will lose out in the end in terms of the time and cost involved in sorting out breakages. The packaging you use and how you pack will depend on your type of work. If your work is very fragile it may be almost impossible to ensure that it is never broken, but with care and thought most objects can be safely packed.

The first essential is that the object(s) are unable to move around in transit. If you are using newspaper as packing material, wet it first so that you can mould it around the object. Bubble-wrap works well as immediate protection but can mark the surface of the work. Polystyrene chips are not good with heavier small items as the objects can work their way to the bottom of the box as it moves around in transit. Boxes within boxes are useful for glass and ceramics; pack the object well in one box, then pack that box well within a second container. If you are packing a number of objects in one package, put light objects inside heavier ones, but never the other way round. Cushion corners with paper, bubble-wrap, sticky tape etc. and take care that they are not too close to the side of the container. For air freighting, wooden containers are not required; toughened cardboard is acceptable. If in doubt, check with the particular air freight company.

You must work on the assumption that all carriers drop packages frequently. If you regularly send work by carrier, make up a test consignment and drop it from height of three feet, kick it a few times and check the result.

There are sometimes restrictions on the packing materials used, for example, your commercial invoices for the USA may have to state that no hay or straw has been included, and newspaper is not permitted as a packing material in consignments for Saudi Arabia. Shipping agents, the DTI, the Chambers of Commerce and embassies can usually advise on any relevant restrictions. Whatever arrangements you make about packing, remember that, in addition to protecting your work, it is also saying something about your business and its image. If you have sent your work abroad it is the way you have taken care of it that the buyer will see first. Don't spoil that first impression because it is inappropriately or inadequately packed.

Taking it yourself

Whatever method of shipping you use, you can handle it all yourself. Remember that within the European Union there are no Customs borders. You can load the car and go, or ship a parcel to Copenhagen or

Calabria as easily as you can to Cheltenham or Carlisle. If you are going to EFTA countries, the European Free Trade Agreement with EU countries means that your work should be duty-free.

You may find it easier and a great deal more interesting to deliver the work yourself. However you travel, once again, allow plenty of time to complete procedures even if your documents are correct. Unlike private travellers, you are shipping cargo and if you arrive at an international border or ferry with minutes to spare you may well find a long queue of lorry drivers getting their papers stamped in front of you. Keep your journey simple, crossing as few borders as possible. Before setting out, investigate the documents you will need. If you are not using a shipping agent to prepare them, the Chambers of Commerce will often be able to give advice. If you ask Customs and Excise, it is best to approach their offices at the port or airport from which you intend to travel. It is unwise to expect British Customs to know other countries' regulations; ask the Customs where you are going what they require. You can contact their Embassy in London or consulates around the country if necessary.

If you are taking a van with goods, you may be able to clear Customs at your final destination. It will be necessary for the vehicle to be closed with an official seal (either at a Customs office at the port of departure or at a major city) but means you can make a "transit clearance" through the frontier customs where delays tend to be longest. If you are travelling to a major trade fair or exhibition you may also find that they have arranged temporary custom facilities at the site.

Shipping by post and by courier

Considering the quantities likely to be involved, sending work by post is an easy way of getting pieces abroad. Although the limit for a single parcel is usually 10 kg, this can sometimes be increased to 20 kg. The limit for letter post is 2 kg. You will almost always find it easier and cheaper to send several parcels by post, rather than one large consignment by other methods. You can insure parcels, usually to a limit of £600, and even send them COD (cash on delivery). Customs procedures are simplified, and a postal receipt acts as your proof of export if you are registered for VAT or need to re-import the work.

Even for a single occasion, it is worth buying the Post Office Guide, available at any main Post Office. It gives all the packing and sealing specifications, details about permitted sizes and weights, customs procedures, together with services such as insurance and cash on delivery. Information is given on each country and its customs requirements, as well as the prohibitions and restrictions on items sent by post.

If you send work by post regularly, you can get special multipart forms with all the necessary customs and record copies you need from companies such as Postabroad (see end of chapter). Otherwise consult the Guide and ask for the forms you need at the Post Office. It will save time when posting work to use main post offices.

For smaller or lighter consignments international courier services are increasingly useful. Although more expensive than the post they are fast and reliable. They have the important advantage that for international deliveries most companies will pay any duty necessary and invoice you in sterling in the United Kingdom. This means that you may well be able to quote a delivered, duty paid price in the currency of the country for all your work. Being able to offer a price on which the buyer knows there will be no additional charges can give you a significant competitive advantage. Information about speed of delivery and charges can be supplied on the telephone and that is how collections are booked. So look in the telephone directory for United Parcels Service (U.P.S.), Federal Express, DHL and the other courier companies.

SHIPPING AGENTS AND PROCEDURES

However you ship your work, unless you are staying within the European Union, you will require Export/Import Documentation. Even within the EU you would be well advised to include a detailed packing list or itemised list of what you are carrying if you are taking it yourself. The paperwork can be time-consuming and occasionally complex. Certainly on the first occasion it can seem complex! If you are not clear about the procedures, get help. International shipping is a very specialised activity and you may find the services of a shipping agent are worth their fee.

The forms you require and the circumstances in which they are used vary with the work, the country to which it is going, the method of shipping, and often with the value of the consignment. Little documentation is required to ship work out of this country. It is principally needed by Customs for our export statistics. (Yes, you are making a contribution to the balance of payments!) However, you may need proof that you have exported work. In the absence of export documents giving such proof, VAT can be charged on re-imported work. Whether you are registered for VAT or not makes no difference and few things are more galling than paying tax to get your own work back into the country.

Other than by post or courier company, the cheapest method of shipping work is consolidated with other consignments travelling by road. This option is largely limited to Europe, although there are services going further afield. Many shippers run scheduled services. A little investigation will identify carriers going to, or near, your required destination. Shippers then use local carriers to make the final delivery if it is not on their normal route. Carriers are listed in the telephone book and will tell you where they go; remember they need the size and weight of your consignment to give you a quote. You must be well organised enough to fit in with their timings for scheduled services – they are not going to wait for you.

Carriage by air is easily organised. It has the advantage of avoiding transit procedures, so that a flight from London to Tokyo is considered a direct British-Japanese frontier crossing. Customs and cargo procedures at all major airports are computerised and the air waybill used for air cargo is most comprehensive, covering shipping costs, insurance charges and other details. As a document of carriage it is the proof that your work has been exported, and is often used as evidence that payment is due for what has been supplied. Do not confuse air cargo with the baggage which you take yourself on a plane. The procedures are not the same. Airline staff will usually help with the paperwork for air cargo, although not the packing, provided that you have got the necessary additional documents. Air freight is charged either by weight or by volume, whichever is the larger. To allow for a very large but light consignment, the carriers will use a formula to calculate a nominal "weight by volume". If it is larger than the actual weight, it is on the nominal weight that you will be charged. You can get information of flights and a quote for the cost of air freight by ringing any appropriate airline cargo office.

Unaccompanied carriage of goods by sea is potentially the slowest method. Unless you have exceptionally heavy or large objects, or a very large quantity of work, the time taken to send goods by sea, plus the necessary trans-shipment via other types of transport to and from the ports, means that you can almost certainly find quicker and simpler methods of shipping. Cargo has to be entered on the ship's bill of lading, which, like the deeds to a house, is one of the few documents still considered a document of title; the holder of a bill of lading owns the goods. Additional paperwork may be necessary to cover payment and clarify the point at which the consignment becomes the purchaser's property, and you should probably ask a shipping office to help with this paperwork.

Any shipping agent or international carriers can organise your shipping and handle the necessary documentation, but it may be worth considering those specialising in the shipment of antiques and works of art (see end of chapter). Shipping is a very competitive business, so ask for several quotes.

Documentation

The principal document you will require is a commercial invoice. This is a comprehensive typed list of everything taken (or sent), if possible on your headed paper. You will need at least three copies. It should be headed "Commercial Invoice" and show your name and address as supplier and the name and address of where the consignment is going. All work must be described in sufficient detail for it to be easily identified, with the number sent if multiples and their unit cost, the materials used and possibly also sizes and making techniques involved. The wholesale value of the work must be shown (not the final selling price). If you are referring to an FOB or C & F order, you must show the quoted price including transport costs. It is on this figure that any tax or duty payable will be calculated. You cannot simply list "six works of art", you must describe each piece, giving its title if appropriate and the date made. You can then add a declaration that the listed items are "original works of art", although some countries will require additional information before accepting them as such. Finally the invoice must be signed with an original, not photocopied, signature.

The commercial invoice may also have to include supplementary information, such as statements regarding the type of packing or that the goods meet necessary safety standards. You should number it as other documents may need to refer to it. Together with the document of carriage (for example, the air waybill), it guarantees what you as exporter have sent and the price you should be paid.

Typical paperwork for a single consignment, whether taken by yourself or sent by a shipping agent, will therefore be :

– a commercial invoice
– a document of carriage (e.g. air waybill)
– certificate of origin or value – if required

If your work is going to an exhibition or trade fair outside the EU and will definitely be returning, you use an ATA Carnet. No invoices are required and the document gives duty- and tax-free passage across all frontiers. It needs no other paperwork or shipping agents (although you can delegate its use to them) and once issued incurs no additional costs. It is simple to use but does take time to prepare. Carnets are issued by Chambers of Commerce. The Carnet requires a guarantee from your bank that tax and duty up to the maximum sum liable will be paid if you do not bring all the work back. Naturally the bank will charge you for giving that guarantee, although the amount will depend upon the value of the goods. Like the commercial invoice, the Carnet is a detailed list of everything being shipped, with weights and values. A copy of the list is provided for each frontier crossed. The simplest Carnet therefore requires four copies – out of and back into this country and into and out of the other. A copy is removed at each frontier and when the consignment returns the Carnet is cancelled by the issuing Chamber of Commerce and the bank withdraws its guarantee. Remember that you cannot vary the procedure and decide to sell some of the work abroad. If you default on the terms of the Carnet, the procedures operate automatically and duty in full will be paid against your bank guarantee. You could be faced with other charges, and a lengthy and potentially expensive process to cancel the Carnet and any balance of the guarantee.

However, if you are sure work will be returning, despite the costs, the ATA Carnet is much the easiest method to use.

Be careful if your documents do not have a specific destination for your work. You may have loaded the car for a general selling trip, but this can cause extra problems which have nothing to do with Customs Duty. In Germany "itinerant selling" currently requires a permit and in other European countries you will be considered a commercial traveller. You may therefore have to consider restrictions which apply to sales in other countries. The DTI have useful booklets giving hints to exporters for most applicable countries and detailed information about itinerant selling. If you are taking pieces speculatively or on a sale-or-return basis, you may be faced with some unexpected charges.

For each method, whether you are using an agent or handling the shipping yourself, the basic documents are the same. It is probably a good idea to use an agent on the first occasion at least. It will give you the confidence to appreciate that shipping is not as difficult as it may seem.

Further reading

The book 'Selling and Exhibiting Abroad' by Judith Staines (AN Publications) provides further information.

Department of Trade & Industry - General Enquiries office
1 Victoria Street
London SW1H 0ET
0171 215 5000
(regional offices in Birmingham, Bristol, Cambridge, Guildford, Leeds, Liverpool, London, Manchester,Newcastle-upon-Tyne, Nottingham, Cardiff, Glasgow and Belfast)

Customs and Excise
Offices throughout the country. Check the telephone directory.
Head office: New Kings Beam House
22 Upper Ground
London SE1 9PJ
0171-626 1515

Postal Export Documentation Sets are available from:

" Postabroad "
Formecon Services Ltd
Gateway
Crewe
Cheshire
CW1 1YN
01270 500800

Information point for questions on export trade transactions:

SITPRO (Simpler Trade Procedures Board)
151 Buckingham Palace Road
London SW1W 9SS
Help Desk 0171 215 0800
Fax 0171 215 0824

British Standards Institution
Technical Help to Exporters (THE)
389 Chiswick High Road
London W4 4AL
0181 996 7111
Assists exporters with foreign regulations, interpreting foreign standards and other requirements.

Shipping agents and carriers See under "Shipping and forwarding agents" in Yellow Pages. Those regularly handling antiques and works of art include:

Pitt & Scott Ltd
60 Coronation Road
London NW10 7PX
0171 607 7321

James Bourlet Inc. UK Ltd.
Unit 06 Beta Way, Thorpe Industrial Park, Crabtree Road
Egham, Surrey, TW20 8RE
01784 470000

Promotion and Publicity

It is fair to assume that most craftspeople want the public to know about their work; publicity is the key to bringing this about, and is an important element in the selling process. As craftwork is essentially about a person making things, it is not often possible to publicise the work without also promoting the maker. Some people dislike this personality cult, but it is important to recognise that there is great public interest in craftspeople – how they live and how they work – and the media will often insist on covering you as well as your work.

There are two types of publicity; ongoing publicity, which is keeping you and your work in the public eye, and specific publicity, such as for an exhibition, open workshop or launch of a new range of work.

The first step is to decide how much time and money you are going to spend on publicity and promotion. It is such an important aspect of your work that you should allocate a fixed percentage of your annual overheads; if you do not promote your work, it will be more difficult to sell. By allowing a fixed percentage, your promotional budget will increase as sales increase. The hope is that a little publicity at the start (when you do not have much cash available) will help your work sell a little better and therefore allow a bit more cash for publicity, leading to even better sales.

Promotional material

Even if you only have a little cash, there is certain basic material which you must have before you can start promoting your work and seeking press coverage. What you need will depend on how and where you plan to sell your work. What is required by someone mainly working to commission may be different from someone selling mostly via galleries and shops. Given that all promotional material costs money to produce, you should think hard about what is likely to be most effective for you.

Photographs

Every craftsman and woman will require photographs of their work and the importance of good-quality photographs of your work is emphasised throughout this book. In the case of the press, your photographs will be competing for limited space alongside professionally taken pictures, so poor photographs are just a waste of time and money. Both black-and-white prints and 35mm colour slides are needed for press and other promotion as is discussed later.

Business Card

This is basically a printed card with your name, address and telephone number, which can be given to all contacts.

Business Cards are particularly relevant to those who are working to commission or selling through major trade or craft fairs. A business card should reflect your work to some extent, and you should make sure that it is well designed and professionally printed. If you are skilful at design and the preparation of artwork, the only cost will be having it printed. If you do not have these skills, then employ a graphic designer. If you decide a postcard (see below) is a higher priority and it contains your name and contact address/telephone number, then this can substitute for a business card.

Headed note paper

As was stated in the chapter on administration, headed note paper can be used as the basis for all your paperwork and well-designed headed paper can emphasise your professionalism and the quality of your work. It is sensible for the design of your note paper and business card to be complementary.

168 POSTCARD

In recent years colour postcards have become one of the most effective methods for publicity and as well as being valuable in promoting your work these can be sold. Many small printers specialise in reproducing a 35mm or larger format colour transparency as a postcard; usually a run of 1000 although some companies now offer runs of 250 or 500 which may be more suitable given that the image can date. The cost is about £60 for 500 cards and £120 for 1000 cards. One side of the card shows a colour photograph of your work, the other side will normally have details of the work on the front, your name, contact telephone number, address and, where relevant, the photographer's credit.

Additional information can be included such as details about your work, your C.V., a map of how to get to your workshop, an invitation to an exhibition, or even Christmas greetings. With print runs of 1000 you can arrange to have some cards printed with more information and the rest with just the basic photo details, name, address and telephone number or left blank. The more cards you have printed the less the cost, so it may be worth considering having extra blank cards printed for later use and for sale. If you intend to sell postcards of your work through shops which stock your work, remember not to put your address and telephone number on the printed material as otherwise the shop will probably refuse to sell them in case customers start approaching you directly to buy work.

To find suitable postcard printers, look in Artist's Newsletter or ask the Crafts Council. For a postcard you require an original unpublished 35mm slide (or larger format which will give better quality). As the postcard will cost you money, and given its value in promoting you and your work, it is sensible to ensure that you use the best image available. It can be worth employing a professional photographer to ensure that the card does your work justice.

Type the information (and double check for accuracy) for the back of the postcard on a blank sheet and have the printer typeset this for you. Often a colour proof of the image is provided by the printer. This is useful as it enables you to check in advance that the image on the card will be acceptable. Check if a proof is normally provided. If not it is worth paying the small additional cost to obtain one.

If the resulting cards are badly printed or the quality of the image poorer than in the proof, then do not hesitate to complain and refuse to pay or demand your money back unless they are reprinted to your satisfaction.

Brochure or leaflet

While few craftspeople are in the position to afford the expensive advertising material produced by large companies, recent advances in the printing industry mean that good-quality monochrome and colour printing is now widely available at lower prices than in the past, so it may be worth investigating having leaflets or brochures printed. If you do, make sure that they are well designed and that you know in advance how you plan to use them. Again, if you intend to give them to shops which sell your work, remember not to put your address on the printed material as otherwise the shop will probably refuse to give them out in case customers start buying from you direct.

C.V. (Curriculum Vitae)

An up to date C.V. is an essential part of your promotional package. There is an example on page 18.

Poster

A poster is probably only relevant if you sell direct and want to attract people to your workshop or if you are advertising a specific event such as an exhibition.

Photocopies of previous publicity

You should keep a portfolio of any press coverage you receive, and in certain circumstances good copies of press articles can be worth sending out to prospective clients. Note on each the name of the publication and the date the article appeared before you have the copies made. If the article is in colour, it can be an advantage to have it photocopied in colour.

Editorial coverage

Other chapters in this book deal with promotional aids such as exhibitions and trade fairs, so this chapter will restrict itself to the use of the media for promoting your work. There are basically two types of media publicity: editorial coverage and paid advertising.

Editorial coverage in a serious newspaper or magazine will bring results that could cost thousands of pounds to achieve through purchased advertising, but it is normally only achieved after considerable outlay on promotional material, energy, research and persistence.

Researching your approach

Having organised your promotional material, you must then consider whom to approach. Craftspeople have a strong case for inclusion in local newspapers and magazines, and Features Editors may be responsive to a story about you and your work if you present them with interesting material. On a national level, it is best to approach specialist craft, design and life-style magazines which already cover work similar or relevant to your own. Try looking through different magazines to see if they carry articles on the crafts or craftspeople, or if you might be able to come up with an approach that will interest them. More and more magazines are interested in the crafts, from 'Brides' to 'The Face'. Time spent on research can lead to you finding unusual but valuable coverage. Foreign magazines can also be worth contacting.

How you approach a publication will to some extent depend on what type of coverage you hope to get, so have a strong, clear idea of what it is you do want. It is worth drawing up a detailed list of the coverage you are chasing together with the names of the people you decide to contact. Remember that magazines will want to fit you into the existing structure of their regular features: for example, 'Country Matters' in Vogue covers rural makers, 'Antennae' in Interiors covers new products with a strong design content, and the Women's Page of the Daily Telegraph regularly spotlights individual craftspeople.

Whom to contact

It is very important to direct your press information to the correct person, and this means compiling a personal press list. Your own research into magazines and newspapers will give you important information for this list. Most magazines contain details of who is responsible for each section. If not, you can always ring up the magazine and ask whom you should contact in connection with a specific section. You can also get valuable advice by asking friends, craft shop owners, gallery directors, regional arts board press officers and guilds or other craft bodies for names of relevant journalists who handle particular features or welcome craft information.

Journalists move around frequently, so it is unwise to simply "lift" a press list from someone else as it may be out of date. You can check it by consulting press directories, such as the one published by PIMS (ask in your reference library), which give comprehensive lists of publications together with the names of specialist journalists.

It is helpful to put your press list onto a card index. You will then be able to revise it easily and also make notes on the individual cards about contacts you have made with particular journalists, their likes and dislikes, freelance activities, long-term plans for articles and other information for future reference. If you are having difficulty finding a particular contact, try ringing up the publication and asking the receptionist who would be the best person to approach; if all else fails address the letter to the "Listings Editor." "Features Editor", "Arts Reviewer" or whatever title seems relevant.

Some media coverage results from approaches made by the press (to a body such as the Crafts Council or a regional arts board), so it is vital to keep such organisations supplied with up-to-date photographs, slides and information so that they may act on your behalf if they receive a media approach relevant to your work. Often press deadlines mean that there is no time for them to contact you, and the opportunity will go to those whose material is instantly available.

TIMING YOUR APPROACH

Most people get caught out in their first attempts at publicity by the length of time newspapers, magazines and radio and television programmes need to plan ahead. Magazines which print in colour usually work at least three months ahead; this means that ideally you should contact them four months in advance, and be able to supply colour transparencies and detailed information fairly soon afterwards. This often creates problems, for example, when work for an exhibition is still being made and details of the event are not finalised. But if you want the publicity, you will have to find a way around this, perhaps by supplying photos of existing work similar to the pieces in the exhibition, and taking calculated risks in predicting what can safely be said about the arrangements.

If you are negotiating for a major feature, it is important that you start talking to the magazine as early as possible as the basic contents of an issue will be planned as much as a year ahead. Bear in mind that most magazines start thinking about their Christmas features in July and that you will always stand a better chance with an idea which is related to the seasonal emphasis of the particular magazine. For example, approach fashion writers about sweaters in May for publication in September when they start covering winter clothes. If you are simply hoping to be included in a regular feature, such as Observer "Billboard", Vogue "Notices" or Interiors "Exhibition Diary", the most important thing is to supply a good photograph and clear, accurate, basic information to the correct person in good time.

Magazines which print in black and white usually go to press about six weeks before they appear. Again, features are planned further ahead, so you should discuss this type of coverage with the magazine well in advance. Regular items, such as listings and notebook columns, are usually compiled as close as possible to the press date from whatever material has come into the office – make sure yours is there.

Newspapers are the most flexible and responsive section of the press. For a major feature or article, it is best to approach the relevant journalist about one month in advance. With more straightforward coverage, such as listings, reviews and news items, you need to approach the paper about ten days before the event – too early and they are likely to lose or forget about your material; too late may mean they have already planned to include something else.

Radio can be an important medium for promoting visual work; even though there are no pictures, it can help attract people to your workshop or an event, and get your name more widely known.
The development of local radio has greatly increased access to radio broadcasting, and your local radio station may be worth considering in any publicity campaign. Most radio stations run a number of magazine programmes which cover events of a local nature. Research the name and format of all suitable programmes and approach them individually

with the relevant information about two weeks before the event. They are likely to put your material into a "planner" diary for consideration a few days before broadcast date, so it is a good idea to follow up your initial approach with a telephone call to check that they have the information and to find out whether any coverage is being considered.

National radio operates in the same way, although only events of truly national interest stand a chance of achieving coverage. Do not waste time sending information to national radio stations unless you are convinced that you have a unique and particularly interesting story to offer.

Local television operates in a similar way to local radio, although there is likely to be less airtime available as they also broadcast a large amount of national networked programmes. Research the local magazine programmes which often go out around either side of the six o'clock news, and also the local news slot which will sometimes consider carrying an "art" item if it has a sufficiently interesting storyline. Some regional television stations also run their own arts programmes, although these tend to be seasonal. You need to carry out a fair amount of research to discover which are the relevant programmes, when their broadcast seasons start and finish, who to approach and to do this in sufficient time for your work to be considered.

National television is probably the hardest kind of coverage to achieve: it includes only a small amount of arts broadcasting which is planned far in advance, and arts material has to compete with every other kind of item for inclusion in news and magazine broadcasts. This results in very limited coverage, often of either a sensational or a trivial nature. Timing your approach to television is similar to radio; two weeks in advance is sufficient for a magazine item, but major coverage should be set in motion as early as possible so that the item can be considered as part of the overall planning of a series.

Contacting the press

As with everyone you send information to, whatever you send will be competing with a mass of other information so try to think of imaginative ways to make yours stand out. Aim to send something which a journalist will pin on the notice board instead of just tossing it into the wastepaper basket. When you contact the press you should send either a letter, a press release, an image or a combination of these.

Be concise but interesting. If you have written to the journalist because of an article you have read, it may be worth mentioning your appreciation of it. Explain why you think you and your work are of interest. Attach a postcard or photograph of your work and any other relevant information, but do not send too much. Follow up your letter with a telephone call after a week or so, but if you get a cool reception leave it at that.

PRESS RELEASE

This may sound like a glamourous and mysterious document; in fact, it is only a piece of paper containing concise information relevant to the press.

A press release should cover what, where, why, when, not necessarily in that order. It should start with an eye-catching and interesting first sentence, which will give the recipient an incentive to read on. Sometimes it is possible to give a press release a short title which sums up the general message in the style of a journalistic headline, but take care not to be over-clever.

Remember that journalists are very busy, constantly working under pressure, so they are looking for news or interesting stories. They are unlikely to be interested in details of your aesthetic decisions, although they may well like to know that you have invented a new technique, constructed the largest coiled pot in the UK or been commissioned by a famous person. This apparently trivial approach does not mean that the press are a bad lot; it reflects the fact that they have to persuade their editors to run arts stories against competing claims from sport, gossip, scandal and the crime desk, and that the management's overall concern is to sell newspapers. The technique to adopt at press release stage is to get the journalist interested and encourage him or her to follow up whatever you are promoting, at which stage it will be possible to introduce the writer or broadcaster to the work and take the whole business onto a more serious level.

Press releases should be as short as possible; only the most exceptionally complex exhibition requires more than one side of A4, and it is usually possible to say all that needs saying in three or four short paragraphs. The layout of the press release can also contribute to its effectiveness. You are promoting visual goods, so the choice of paper, the typeface, width of margin and use of colour should all echo your own high standards, as well as presenting the message in a clear and attractive manner. Type the press release in double space as this helps the journalist to include notes as they read it.

You may wish to include some visual reference about the work; some photographs will photocopy effectively and can be used either on the press release itself, or on an attached sheet. If you have a postcard of a piece of work this would be a useful enclosure. It is not necessary, or expected to send out unsolicited press photographs at press release stage.

Every press release should have a "nuts and bolts" section which includes the relevant items from the following list:

- date(s) of event
- place and opening times of event
- admission charges, if any
- availability of press photographs, b/w and/or colour
- availability of work for viewing or for photography
- press preview/viewing arrangements
- availability of catalogue or other written material
- telephone number and name of person to contact for further information

It is difficult to be objective enough about your own work to write an effective press release, so consider asking someone else to write it.

Press photographs

Newspapers or magazines which print in black and white require high quality, high-contrast black and white photographs, which are normally printed on 10 x 8 inch paper. Bear in mind that any photographs you supply will be competing with a lot of other images on the editor's desk. The press cannot reproduce from a black and white photograph which has already been printed, for instance in a catalogue, but require an original print.

The press do not expect to have photographs supplied automatically with a press release. However, journalists do expect a good selection of pictures to be available to them immediately upon request – it is no good saying that your brother-in-law is coming round with his Nikon in ten days' time!

Black & white photographs should always carry a caption, in the form of a typed label attached to the back of the picture, giving details of what is shown in the photo and the photographer's name if he/she should be credited.

EXAMPLE OF CAPTION
Jane Jones completing work on her slate-cut plaque, to be unveiled by HRH The Prince of Wales when he opens Middletown Children's Hospital on Tuesday 14 February
Photo credit: Jim Smith
Please return to Jane Jones, The Old Schoolhouse, Middletown

Colour photographs in magazines and catalogues are taken from colour slides or transparencies, not prints. It is important to try to supply originals, not copy slides, so take, or ask the photographer to take, multiple exposures to give you an adequate supply. 35mm slides give a good quality reproduction and are adequate for most situations. Sometimes large-format transparencies (5in x 4in or larger) are used where particularly high quality is required. Slides should be captioned in the same way as black and white photos. It is a good idea to pack slides in transparent plastic wallets with rows of pockets, available from photographic shops, with the captions typed on labels affixed to the relevant pockets. Put a number on each slide and a matching number on each caption.

Make sure that any photographs which have to be sent by post are packed between sheets of stiff cardboard, or in card-backed envelopes. Always pack slides carefully for posting, particularly if they are mounted between glass.

It is not wise to count on photographs being returned after use; order a good supply in the first instance, regard them as gone, and those which do come back will be a useful bonus.

It is important to be sure that you are not infringing anyone's copyright when you supply photographs to the press, because you imply that you are in a position to grant the right to reproduce them. As a general rule, if you commission photographs it is a good idea to state, in writing, at the start of the transaction that you wish to buy the copyright or have a license to use them for publicity and promotional purposes.

Checking copy

Makers are understandably concerned whether they will have the opportunity to correct copy which is written about them before it is printed. There is no general rule about this, some journalists like to check copy in advance, and others simply do not operate in this way. A sensible compromise is to ask whether you will have the opportunity to check copy, make it as easy as possible for the journalist to reach you, but don't alienate someone who is in a position to help you by making a fuss if it becomes clear that he or she cannot give you advance access to the material.

Paid advertising

Buying advertising space is another way of achieving communication with the readership of a particular publication. All the available research on effective publicity indicates that people respond to a broad range of promotional activity, and an effective campaign will include several different elements which link up with each other to convey an overall message. Few craftspeople or crafts organisations are likely ever to be in a financial position to consider promoting their work through advertising as a primary medium; however, it can have an important role to play in conjunction with other publicity activity.

Classified advertising

This is an inexpensive form of advertising where a newspaper or publication groups announcements of a similar nature together under a generic heading; craftspeople are most likely to be concerned with classified categories for the promotion of exhibitions, ongoing promotion of a workshop sales outlet, a service or a particular object.

Classified advertising is inexpensive and because it can only convey basic information – times, places, dates, names. It relies on other media to persuade the audience of the interest and value of the facility on offer.

Display advertising

This is the term used for advertisements which appear within marked-out panels, individually designed, and either grouped together with other advertisements or interspersed in the text of newspapers or magazines. The cost of advertising is given on the magazine's rate card, supplied on request; major publications list their rates in the directory British Rates and Data (BRAD). Rates for display advertisements vary enormously, and you should find out how many copies the particular publication sells in order to evaluate its effectiveness as an advertising medium. Some small magazines quote you the number of copies which they print rather than the number which they sell, unless correctly questioned, and a smart advertising manager will always tell you the estimated readership, usually much greater than the number of copies distributed on the basis that more than one person will read each copy.

You can compare the advertising value offered by different publications if you divide the cost of the advertising space by the number of people reached.

Directory entries

It is worth keeping an eye on directories, yearbooks and handbooks, particularly if you are trying to promote a particular type of work to a professional group, for example wall hangings to architects. Some directories carry basic entries free, but charge for a fuller listing – read the sales literature carefully. It is unwise to spend money on advertising in a new publication of this type; wait until it has proved itself, and become a known and trusted reference work.

ARRANGING ADVERTISING

Having decided which publications you will advertise with, find out the copy date for the particular issue in which you want to appear. You will then have to prepare the artwork from which the advertisements will be printed. Most art magazines, and many general interest magazines, will design and make up advertisement artwork for a small extra charge. This will be in a compatible style to the rest of the magazine and of professional appearance, but you must not expect to be able to stipulate more than a very general description of how you wish the advertisement to look.

If you want to have greater artistic control over the appearance of your advertisement, you will need to commission a graphic designer or prepare the artwork yourself if you have the necessary experience. But remember that large unionised magazines and newspapers may not carry artwork prepared by non-union designers. You will need a separate piece of artwork for every publication in which you have booked space, it is not realistic to expect to transfer artwork from one publication to another. Artwork should be prepared wherever possible to the exact size of the advertisement space; this is known as "s/s" artwork. If the printers have to enlarge, reduce or carry out any other technical work on your artwork, they will charge extra.

When the advertisement appears, the publisher should send you a copy of the magazine or newspaper, with the bill. This is known as supplying a "voucher copy". These copies are sent out as soon as the publication appears, so that advertisers cannot claim the publication did not occur on time. If you book an advertisement which appears after the event has taken place because the magazine came out late, you are entitled to ask for a reduction as long as the expected publication date was clearly established as part of the original contract between you and the publisher.

 You may wish to use advertising to invite people to send for your brochure, arrange a visit to your workshop, etc. You can assess the effectiveness of your advertising by monitoring the replies. If you are advertising in several publications, you could consider using different names (J. Jones, Jones Knitwear, JJ Knits, Jonwear Knits), thus enabling you to assess the number, type and quality of replies attracted by each which will guide you when placing future advertisements.

Public relations (PR)

PR is a separate area of activity to advertising and publicity, but so closely related that it is necessary to make some comment about its influence. In the simplest terms, PR is your relationship with the outside world. Publicity gobbles up time and money; good PR means that in addition you take the trouble to do things over and above the minimum standard required, exhibiting good grace, energy and enterprise.

Examples of good PR are bothering to make a special journey to deliver press photos at the end of a long day, cancelling a visit to your mother because a writer cannot interview you at any other time, and being cheerful when someone rings up to check details on a piece at eleven o'clock at night. The demands made on you will often be unfair, unreasonable and unrealistic, but if you are readily available, willing and helpful, publicity opportunities will come your way more and more frequently.

Exhibiting

"How do I arrange to have an exhibition of my work?" is a question craftspeople often ask. The main ways are to be asked to exhibit by a gallery, to participate in a Guild or craft group show or to arrange your own exhibition, either alone or in partnership with others.

Being invited to exhibit

The easiest way is to be asked to do so by an established gallery or shop. Of course, this very rarely comes out of the blue and you will usually need to spend time building up contacts and approaching possible galleries about exhibiting your work.

If you are asked to exhibit by a gallery you should take time to consider the invitation before saying yes. Given that it is always flattering to be asked to exhibit it is all too easy to agree to show work and then discover that the venue or exhibition is inappropriate. So if approached by a gallery it is best to say that the offer sounds interesting but that you would like some time to think about it. If you let them know when you will get back to them with a decision and stick to this timetable they are unlikely to be upset if you eventually say no. You need to obtain as much information in advance as you can so that you can make your decision.

The venue

If you do not know the venue personally it is unwise to agree to exhibit there until you have done some research. Ask other makers who have exhibited with the gallery or your Regional Arts Board for their views. Ask the gallery for a list of previous exhibitors, to contact for an opinion.

Solo or Group Exhibition

If it is not to be a solo exhibition then you will want to know what the purpose of the exhibition is, particularly if it is a contextual show in which work is being selected to illustrate an issue or theme as this may affect your view on whether to be included. Who else will have work in the exhibition? Your decision whether to exhibit may be influenced by the fact that someone whose work you dislike is also included or that your greatest influence is one of the exhibitors.

Timescale

When would the show be and how much work would you be expected to provide? How long is the show planned to last and is it to tour? A tour could mean your work being away for a long time but could increase the number of people seeing your work and the possible sales and media exposure.

Working out the cost

Will there would be any cost to you? Check carefully what the gallery will provide and whether there is likely to be some cost to you. You should expect the gallery to pay for transport of the work, insurance, publicity, the catalogue and the private view. However, you should also expect them to take a sizeable commission on sales in return for their promotion of you and your work. Unfortunately we do not live in a perfect world, and in some cases you may discover that the gallery expects you to contribute towards part of the exhibition costs. If you are expected to contribute, then you will have to balance the cost against the possible advantages and decide whether it is worth going ahead. Furthermore, if you have to contribute to the costs, you should expect the gallery to charge less commission on sales. Be clear about who pays for what before agreeing. It may be that certain things are not normally provided unless the exhibitor(s) cover these and you will need to decide in such cases whether or not you are willing to pay.

Even if there is no direct cost to you it is important that you recognise the expense of producing a body of work for an exhibition. In addition you may have to find the cost of attending the opening.

A factor in estimating the final cost to you is whether the work will be for sale and, if so, whether you think it likely that the gallery will be successful in selling your work. Private galleries exist by selling work so they will normally have approached you because they feel your work will sell to their clients. However local art galleries & museums, while willing for the work to be for sale, may lack the expertise to do this successfully.

FUNDING

Some galleries pay a fee to exhibitors and a number of Regional Arts Boards operate a scheme whereby funded galleries have to pay exhibition fees to artists and craftspeople (Exhibition Payment Right) although this normally only relates to shows with up to three exhibitors and is a relatively small amount.

Some galleries buy work in advance as a way of assisting those exhibiting to produce a body of work and this can be worth raising as a possibility with someone approaching you.

Although you are being invited to exhibit it may be possible to obtain a grant for the show. This could be for special promotional material or a catalogue; again check with funding bodies to see if there might be a grant available.

CONTRACT

Once you have agreed to exhibit you should receive a contract or written agreement setting out what each party is required to provide and do. If you receive a contract check to ensure that it covers the relevant points listed below :

– The venue for the exhibition
– Dates of the exhibition and opening times

– Number of pieces and whether new or existing
– When work is to be ready by and delivered
– Who is responsible and will pay for delivery of work to the exhibition and return of unsold work
– Any specific instructions about installation
– Provision of photographs and when required
– What expenses the exhibitor is responsible for (private view, promotional card, etc.)
– What the venue will provide (private view, promotional card, publicity, etc.)
– Who is responsible for insuring the work; in transit and in the gallery
– Whether the work will be for sale and, if so, the gallery's commission on sales

If the gallery does not issue contracts to exhibitors you may wish to consider making up your own and asking the gallery to sign it.

AN Publications publish an example Exhibition Contract in their series of Visual Arts Contracts.

Preparing the exhibition

If you are being asked to exhibit then, unless your work has particular hanging or handling requirements, you usually will not be involved in the organisation of the exhibition except to provide the work and relevant information and photographic material.

Therefore it is important that you are clear about the purpose of the exhibition and how your work will be used within it. There are cases where people agree to exhibit in a show only to find that it was not what they expected. An exhibition may have a thesis which requires the work to be displayed or described in a particular way.

 Once the exhibition is created it can be difficult for the organiser to change anything, although if you are unhappy with the way your work is displayed or described then you should arrange to speak to the organiser to see if a compromise can be reached. If the disagreement is serious and you feel that the way your work is being used is detrimental, then you should consider removing it from the exhibition although this would only be as a last resort and you would need to investigate any contractual agreement that you had with the venue.

Delivery & Insurance

Check that it is clearly agreed who is responsible for the costs of transporting the work, both ways, and for insurance cover in transit and while in the exhibition.

Publicity material

If photographs are required for a private view card, a catalogue or press release then you will need to ensure that you know what you are to provide and by when. You may be presuming that you will be able to make the work at the last minute and suddenly discover that work is required for photography at an earlier stage.

You are likely to have to provide an up to date C.V., a list of the work which will be in the exhibition, prices of work, etc. and some of this may be required well in advance of the opening.

Publicity

Normally the gallery will take responsibility for promoting the exhibition but you may want to discuss what they normally do and whether there is extra work you could do to increase the likelihood of press coverage. You will want to ensure that those on your personal mailing list are sent exhibition information and invitations to any private view.

Press & Private Views

Again this should be the responsibility of the gallery although in some instances you may be asked to pay something towards the private view. Make sure that the people you want to be at the Private View are invited.

During the exhibition

You may want to discuss with the gallery whether it would be useful for you to run special activities during the exhibition; such as workshops for schools or other groups or talks about your work as ways of promoting the exhibition.

It can be useful to have photographs of the exhibition in situ taken as a record.

Afterwards

After the exhibition is finished you will need to find out if any work has been sold and, if so, invoice the gallery. Any unsold work will need to be returned or collected.

It is worth asking the gallery to supply names and addresses of anyone who bought work or expressed interest in your work so that you can add them to your own private mailing list for future exhibitions, although you may have to accept that certain galleries will refuse to provide this information.

Ensure that you get archive copies of any publicity material such as poster, private view card, catalogue or whatever, for your records.

Finally try to get feedback from the gallery on how they felt the exhibition and your work was received.

Organising your own exhibition

For those who are not approached by galleries in this way, the alternative is to do it yourself. However, do consider whether the time spent organising your own show might not be better used in pursuing the contacts which could lead to an established gallery inviting you to exhibit.

Putting on your own exhibition is likely to involve a great deal of work, financial outlay and some panic. As with most things, organising an exhibition seems relatively straightforward to those who have previous experience whereas to those attempting it for the first time it can appear a minefield. It need not be so. By talking to people who are involved in exhibition organisation, you can quickly gather the basic know-how.

AN Publications publish 'ORGANISING YOUR EXHIBITION' by Debbie Duffin which provides fuller information on organising your own exhibition.

SELECTING A VENUE

What is the primary purpose of organising your own show? Is it to sell your work, to gain general publicity, to interest people in commissioning work from you, for prestige, or merely to add a useful line to your c.v.? In most cases, of course, an exhibition will involve more than one of these purposes but you should decide the primary reason in order to choose what type of venue to go for.

If you are content to have a small show involving a few selected objects, then it may be worth exploring the possibility of using building society or bank windows in your area. Such organisations often make their windows available free of charge. A few objects interestingly displayed, combined with well-laid-out information about your work (including prices), where it can be bought and a contact address, can be a relatively cheap way to promote your work.

Another possibility is to see if your local library has one or two display cases which you could use for a small show. An extension of this idea might be to fix up a number of different venues and arrange a small tour of the show. For example, two weeks in four different venues would increase the number of people seeing your work for minimal effort.

If you wish your exhibition to be more than a small selection of objects, one useful area to explore is local authority galleries. Many of these receive no additional funds to mount exhibitions, so those in charge may be glad of the chance to show some craftwork at no cost to the gallery. Some may charge, some may provide free space, while others may offer space plus other facilities. In addition to local authority galleries, it is also worth investigating those attached to local educational establishments. Other possibilities include small private galleries, which can often be hired, and the foyer spaces of public buildings such as libraries, theatres and concert halls.

In choosing a space, remember to take into account the facilities available, such as lighting, display cases (important where these are essential for the security of your work), public accessibility, etc. and balance these against any cost of hiring. A useful publication for help in finding an exhibition venue is DIRECTORY OF EXHIBITION SPACES, published by AN Publications.

SOLO OR GROUP EXHIBITION

Having chosen the venue, you need to decide whether the exhibition should be of your work alone or involve others. This choice will be based partially on preference and partially on circumstances. You know your own preference; what about circumstances? The main point to take into account is the certain saving in time and money gained by sharing an exhibition. But savings will only come about if those joining together in the exhibition carefully divide the cost and workload before beginning the arrangement. In dividing the workload, take care to allocate tasks to those most suited to carry them out. There is little point in making the shyest member responsible for press contact, or in giving charge of finances to the person whose workshop drawer is renowned for its collection of unpaid, coffee-stained invoices, crumpled tax demands and assorted recipes for glazes.

Working out the cost

Before deciding whether to organise an exhibition, you will need to assess if you can afford to do this, be it by yourself or sharing with others. List the areas of likely expenditure, and then estimate what each will cost or what you can afford.

If you are unsure of the costs, it can be helpful to talk to a gallery or to someone who has organised an exhibition before. It is also useful to get a few estimates for such costs as catalogue printing, posters, etc. The main areas of expenditure might include hire of the gallery, special display, hire of cases, insurance, transport, photography, posters, catalogue, leaflets, publicity, postage, telephone and a private view. If there is possible income from catalogue sales or fees from participants, then that can help to offset the expenditure. Once you know the likely cost, you will be able to see how feasible the exhibition is and assess whether to go ahead.

It may be possible to obtain some grant aid towards mounting the exhibition from your Regional Arts Board or the Welsh or Scottish Arts Councils (depending on where you live) and it is worth contacting the appropriate officer to find out if the project would be eligible. If you are ineligible to apply as an individual or group, then you could see whether it would be possible for the venue to apply for part of the costs on your behalf.

If you wish to apply for a grant, remember that the funding body will need plenty of time to consider your application and that there will be some delay between applying and being advised if your application has been successful.

Sponsorship is another possibility although it can be particularly hard for individuals to raise sponsorship. Sponsors are normally looking to put money into events from which they will gain publicity or prestige so it is unlikely that larger companies will assist a small exhibition. However local businesses might be interested and you could try asking for helping in kind rather than direct funding; for example a donation of paper for the catalogue or free wine for the private view. Sponsorship is often decided by someone in the company who has a particular interest in an event so it can be worth researching if you, or your relations, know anyone in a relevant company who might have influence.

The timing and length of the exhibition

With the venue agreed and the composition of the exhibition sorted out, the next step is to fix a date. Organising an exhibition takes time so do not plan the date three months ahead if it will take you three months to make the actual pieces to be exhibited, for you will find the time required for organisational details conflicts with the making. If your time scale does not adequately allow for both the making of work and the organisation of the exhibition, then postpone the date. Remember too that you may need to allow time for a grant application or to raise the money from other sources.

The length of the exhibition will often be fixed by the venue, but do ensure that it is neither so short that publicity and word of mouth have no time to take effect, nor so long that it puts a burden on your time and finances. In general, two weeks is the minimum length and one month the maximum. The length is particularly relevant if you are having to staff the show for security reasons.

Display

Display is crucial. There is little point in spending time creating fine objects if these are then badly displayed. You will need to visit the venue in advance so that you can check what is available. Does the venue have any special display equipment, plinths or cases, as if not you may need to borrow or hire these; is the lighting provided adequate for your purposes; are there are any regulations which may make it impossible for you to hang or display work in the way you had planned?

It can be useful to get a plan of the space (or make your own) so that you can spend time in advance thinking about how best to display your work in the space. Display is one area where imagination and care can compensate to a great extent for a shortage of cash.

A dowdy display will ruin even the best object and you must ensure that walls, stands, display cases, etc. are freshly painted or cleaned. Do not forget to check the display regularly throughout the period of the exhibition as grubby fingers and dust can ruin the original effect.

Labelling exhibits gives a professional feel to the exhibition. Labels should be typed (unless your craft is calligraphy) and mounted on thick card which will not curl; include the maker's name (if a group show), the date of making, details of the medium/process, the catalogue number (if any), the owner (if borrowed) and the selling price. Mounted photographs and information panels on the maker(s) can add to the professional feel of the show.

Title of the exhibition

Given that your exhibition will be trying to attract the attention of the public and the press, it is worth considering what to call the exhibition. The title can be informative or catchy, depending on the audience you hope to attract. However, do remember that such titles as "An Exhibition of New Work by Jones and Smith" will not necessarily mean much to those who do not know what Jones and Smith make. So make sure that the title indicates what will be on show.

Insurance & Security

Insurance must be thought about, unless the venue provides this as part of the cost. Security may also have to be considered and often this will involve someone being on hand to keep an eye on the exhibits. If the work on display is valuable or easily removed then you should ensure that two people are on duty at all times as it is easy for one person on their own to be distracted. Thefts from exhibitions are not uncommon and this possibility needs to be considered.

Publicity

Publicity is essential but this is an area where money and time can easily be wasted. First, consider carefully what you would like the publicity to do. Having decided that, try to direct your publicity effort to the most suitable places. Press coverage is free publicity but in order to obtain such coverage a lot of patient effort must be expended. See the previous chapter for information on obtaining editorial coverage.

A poster can be useful but expensive. One possibility is to combine the poster with the catalogue as a broadsheet so that the print run is extended and savings made by not having to do the two separately. Take care that the size of the poster is right for the sites where it is to be displayed: too large and some will refuse to put it up; too small and it may not be noticed by anyone. A3 or Crown is probably the right size.

Whether or not to have a catalogue will, to a great extent, be decided by the cash you have available. A catalogue is basically a list of the exhibits, although it can be expanded to become much more. For instance, you could ask a critic or 'name' whom you know admires your work or who has bought a piece in the past to write about your work for your catalogue. This can enhance your reputation and bring additional publicity and sales.

A possible alternative (in addition to the idea of a combined poster/ catalogue broadsheet just mentioned) is to have a brochure printed giving information on you and your work which, when combined with a simple typed list of exhibits, will work as a catalogue and will also be useful after the exhibition for general promotion.

Similarly, if you want to have a special private view card printed, one idea might be to have a postcard with a colour photograph on one side and private view information on the other. By extending the print run with the private view information omitted, you could provide yourself with blank postcards showing one piece of your work for little extra cost. Such cards often sell well at exhibitions.

Remember to check that the copy for any poster, publicity leaflet, invitation card or press release includes the title of the exhibition, the venue's address, the period of exhibition, the times of opening and admission charges (if any). The date and time of any private view must also be included on the invitation card and the press release. It is essential that copy is carefully checked (several times) as a mistake on basic details can cause embarrassment and confusion.

Care should also be taken to include any acknowledgements on publicity material where this is required (for example, "subsidised by South West Arts", "with the help of the Gresham Company").
All invitations to the private view should go out at least a fortnight before the actual date.

Press Views

If you are holding an exhibition or special event, you may wish to hold a press view. This is by no means obligatory, and it is better not to do it unless you have reason to be confident that sufficient people will turn up to prevent it being an embarrassment. The reason for holding a press preview is to give journalists an opportunity to see the work in advance of the general public, and to speak to the maker(s) away from all the commotion of a normal private view.

However, few small exhibitions are likely to attract a sufficient number of journalists and it is probably more sensible to invite them to the private view, with the offer of a quiet look round beforehand or at a specific time on the first day of the show. If you do decide to hold a press preview, the best time is the lunch time preceding the opening day of the exhibition, with the private view in the evening. Check whether any other press events are taking place at the same time; it can be an advantage to tie in with a relevant event in a nearby venue, but a disaster if all the journalists are at a competing event on the other side of town. The press normally ignore RSVP requests, but if you want to have some indication of attendance in advance a separate pre-addressed reply card will produce some results. It is normal to provide wine or other drinks at a press preview and sometimes snacks or a buffet lunch. People do not write reviews as a result of a few plates of sandwiches, but providing refreshments can be a way of extending a hospitable welcome to members of the press, whose help you are hoping to receive.

Arrange for someone to be at the entrance to the gallery to welcome journalists and ask them to sign the visitor's book; this enables you to find out who people are. Have on display a full set of press photographs which can be handed out on request. It is a good idea for a note to be made of those who take photographs as this will help you look out for subsequent coverage. You may also wish to provide complimentary catalogues or any other supporting information.

After the preview, look through the visitor's book and establish whether there are any journalists you (realistically) hoped would attend but did not. It is still possible to write or telephone to say how sorry you were that they were unable to make the preview and encourage them to visit the exhibition during the normal opening period. However, do learn to take "no" for an answer and gracefully let the matter drop if you are obviously making no headway.

PRIVATE VIEW

If you are arranging a private view and wish to extend the range of people invited, it is worth asking the venue, other galleries, local art and design colleges, your regional arts association and other craft and art organisations for suggestions or lists. Do take care, however, not to duplicate invitations or to invite too many people. Other gallery and shop owners/directors can be worth inviting as they may be impressed enough to offer you a show at their gallery. Regional Arts Boards and Crafts Council staff should also be included. Even if none of these come to the private view, some may well come along to the exhibition later. A private view can also be a good way of thanking people who have helped – your bank manager again – and do not forget to invite friends and relations. Your Aunt Eliza may very well be the first person to buy something and so encourage a rash of red spots.

As with the press view, arrange for someone to be at the entrance to the gallery to welcome people and ask them to sign the visitor's book.

AFTERWARDS

When the exhibition is over, send letters of thanks to anyone who has helped or lent work. Figures for attendance and catalogue sales (if known) may be worth recording (if you have received a grant this may be a condition of the support) and copies of all publicity material carefully kept as a record. A final account of the income and expenditure relating to the exhibition is worth drawing up, and this will be essential if any grants have been received. Send a copy of the accounts and a report on the exhibition to all those who gave financial assistance.

And what will be the result of all your work and sleepless nights? All your work sold? Gallery owners clamouring to promote your next show? More commissions than you can handle? Photographs of your work in every colour magazine? Your overdraft repaid? Well, perhaps not, but hopefully some work will have sold, contacts will have been made and your work more widely seen.

Exhibiting in a guild or craft group exhibition

Many craft guilds and organisations organise exhibitions of members work and these can be a useful source of publicity and sales. Normally these are organised by the members with those participating involved in some or all aspects of the exhibition organisation.

The points already covered relate to these exhibitions as well and the important thing, again, is to be clear in advance what you will be expected to contribute in time and money.

Photography

As is stated throughout this book, it is essential to ensure that your work is represented by images of the highest quality. Although photographs/slides can only give an approximate representation of work it is through seeing a photograph that many people may first experience your work. It is essential that your photographs do justice to your work as poor images are a waste of time and money.

It can be worth asking someone who knows your work and whose views you value if they think that your photographs or slides do your work justice. Given that you are very close to your work, it can be hard to be objective and an image you feel to be inappropriate may appear a particularly effective image to others.

Many grant or exhibition applications are judged through slides and it is important to try to give yourself time to ensure that you have ones with which you are satisfied. Receiving your slides back from the photographer a day before a deadline and discovering they are dreadful is not a happy experience. Having to decide whether to send poor slides which you know do not do your work justice or miss out on that opportunity is a dilemma without a satisfactory solution.

However as it is useful to ensure that you should try to have a photographic record of all your work, better to have a less than perfect photograph/slide of a piece which you have just finished and is going off to a buyer or an exhibition from which it may be sold, than to end up with no record at all.

Deciding on the image

It is important to decide how you wish your objects to be photographed as the particular image will affect the way your work is viewed. Different contexts demand different photographic approaches. For a grant application simple shots may be best while the same object may need a radically different photograph for submission to a life-style magazine. Objects can look quite different depending on the way they are photographed or lit or set.

Look at images of craft objects in slide indexes, catalogues and magazines to get ideas as to how your objects might best be photographed. Be aware of how your view of the object is affected by the overall image; the photograph of a splendid knitted jacket may be less effective if worn by a relation with no modelling experience.

You may require different types of images of the same object. Someone who makes textiles may need to have photographs of details to send with a grant application and others of the textiles worn by a model for use in fashion magazines. If you are having details photographed, it is sensible also to photograph the complete object as someone who does not know your work will find it easier to understand the detail if there is also a photo of the complete object.

Ensure that the object is photographed to a reasonable scale – while some space around the work is normally helpful too much space usually means a small reproduction of the actual object which is difficult to read properly.

Although many craftspeople are ambivalent about including themselves in photographs, images of you in your workshop, making work or with a finished piece can be useful for press publicity, reports, etc.

Type of Photograph

You will need to decide which kind of photographs you require.

BLACK & WHITE

Black and white prints are useful for newspapers and magazines, catalogues, portfolios, etc. These should be high quality with medium-contrast and are normally printed on 10" by 8" glossy paper. Colour prints can be useful for portfolios and for promotional purposes. However prints are inappropriate for reproduction in magazines and catalogues.

35MM SLIDES

35mm transparencies (slides) are essential for submissions for grants, inclusion in slide indexes, talks about your work, etc. and can be used for colour reproduction as postcards and in magazines, catalogues, brochures, etc. When slides are being reproduced it is essential that an original is used. Thus ensure that you take or have taken a number of shots of the same image if you think it may be reproduced a number of times.

LARGER FORMAT TRANSPARENCIES

Sometimes large format transparencies (5" x 4" or larger) are required where particularly high-quality reproduction is required.

Doing It Yourself

This section is written by Ian Dobbie, who has photographed the Crafts Council Collection.

To produce a good photograph of a piece of work, four fundamental points must be borne in mind. The first and most important is the quality of light. Second comes the viewpoint, i.e. the position of the camera and the lens to be used. Third, the choice of background. Finally, the exposure of the image onto the film.

LIGHTING

To avoid the technical complexities and expense of artificial lighting, use daylight. When correctly managed, it is easy and costs nothing. Most photographs should be attempted indoors, but if a very large piece of work has to be photographed outside, avoid very sunny or windy days. Also, no matter how cloudy it is, keep the position of the sun to the left or right and slightly behind the camera.

Indoors, work as near as possible to the largest available window. First, tape over the windowpane with tracing paper: this will diffuse the daylight, remove hard shadows and reduce troublesome contrast. Then, place a table-top or large flat surface up against the window-sill. Next, place your object to face the camera, with the window to the right or left front of the object; this will throw a soft side-light across it, illuminating whatever you decide are its favourable characteristics. Finally, obtain the largest manageable sheets of white card and place them as near as possible in order to reflect light back onto the object's shadow side.

Camera Lens

The single lens reflex camera of most makes, at reasonable price, will give good results. Failing that, a 'sure-shot' (automatic focus) range finder type is a little more tricky but will just about do. The lens on the camera is important. Fortunately the 'standard' lens (50mm) supplied with most cameras will do for most objects. However, close-up work, for example of jewellery, really needs an 85mm or 100mm lens, together with a close focusing accessory costing only a few pounds called a diopter. Finally, the camera must be fixed rigidly in the taking position by a tripod, which is an essential piece of equipment. But if it proves too expensive, you might use a camera clamp to fix the camera to a sturdy chair.

Background

The backgrounds below and behind the object need thought. Anything too highly coloured or textured could be distracting. Choose a neutral light tone, off-white rather than pure white. Avoid black, unless the object is virtually all one light tone and has a striking profile. Cloth makes a cheap and seamless background; try linen, canvas or even a double bedsheet ironed smoothly.

Film

Choose a colour transparency film that is 'balanced' or sensitized for use in daylight. The transparency or 'slide' gives a positive image which can be used for projecting, printing and reproducing in publications. If more than one transparency is needed, it is best to make them all at the same time in the camera, rather than going for a laboratory-made duplicate later on; which will not only be expensive but of poorer quality because it is a copy. The brand of film is not so important, but it should be rated at 64 to 100ASA. If black and white prints are required then use a negative film rated at 125ASA.

Taking the photograph

The most important thing to consider when taking the picture is how the exposure is measured. Most cameras have a built-in light meter to do this. Its decisions are not always satisfactory, so a series of exposures above and below the camera's recommended setting must also be taken. If the camera is not fully automatic, this is relatively easy.

First, set the lens aperture to f.11 (or f.16 for increased sharpness). Then as indicated by the camera meter set the shutter speed for a 'correct' exposure. After taking a photograph (exposure) at this setting and without altering the shutter speed, rotate the aperture ring selecting half-stop positions to make three exposures both above and below the first setting. This will mean that with f.11 as the start position a total of seven exposures are made ranging from f.7 to f.18.

For a fully automatic camera it must first be set up so that the lens is using a small aperture such as f.11 or f.16. Then, simply vary the exposures by rotating the camera's own exposure compensating dial, moving from its + to - position, again by half-stop increments.

Producing clear sharp images of your work will require the lens setting to be at its smallest apertures. Even on a bright day this will require the use of slow shutter speeds; typically of ¼ to 1 second duration. Now you can understand the need for a sturdy tripod.

The resulting transparencies will show a transition from too dark to too light. One will be correct. Remember that if you require a number of originals of the same shot, you will need to take that number at each aperture setting so that you have the required number of originals of the one that is correct.

Using these techniques will enable a high technical standard to be achieved in 35mm photography. These hints are very basic but, if you want to, they could help produce both creative and inventive images.

Commissioning a professional

The important thing is to try and track down the most appropriate photographer for your work within your budget. At best try and use a photographer whom you know to have experience of taking photographs of your particular craft discipline and whose work you know and like. If you do not know someone ask other makers in your field for recommendations. It may be that you come across someone who is not known to others and in such instances it is advisable to ask to see some photographs of three dimensional work they have done previously before going ahead.

THE COST

Professional photographers can be expensive but if you obtain an excellent set of photos a large outlay can be worth it. Some craftspeople have swapped work with photographers in lieu of payment and if a photographer admires your work this might be worth discussing.

 Having worked out what you require (see next section) you should then discuss what the cost is likely to be and whether the fee quoted includes all expenses, cost of film processing, prints and/or slides, etc.

Giving clear instructions

It is important that you give clear instructions to the photographer about what you want. Things to clarify might include:

- How many objects you wish photographed
- Whether you wish details and/or full shots
- Whether you wish multiple 35mm shots of certain objects for reproduction purposes
- Which kinds of format you require
- The purpose of the photographs – are they for your own record or for a particular magazine, catalogue, etc.
- Any preferences in the way the objects will be lit, backgrounds, their scale within the photograph, etc.

Copyright

It is important to be clear about copyright. Under the new laws on copyright, photographers own the copyright in their photographs unless they pass the copyright to someone else in writing. If you are not being given copyright, then you need to ensure that you obtain permission to use the photographs and to send them to magazines, slide indexes, etc. for reproduction.

While this can be given orally it is wise to ask the photographer to put in writing their consent for you to use the photographs for all your purposes. This is important, for if you send a photograph to a magazine you need to have the photographer's permission for the image to be used for this purpose. When you send out photographs or slides you should credit the photographer in the caption.

Remember that where you have commissioned photographs and feel that they have neither been taken in the way that you discussed nor think they are satisfactory, discuss this with the photographer to see if the photographs should be retaken or the fee reduced.

Captioning photographs

All your photographs should be captioned. With prints stick a typed label to the back. For 35mm slides and transparencies, label each one with your name and give it a number and on a separate sheet or on labels on the transparency pack list the number with the materials used, size, date made, etc.

Example of caption for record/application/exhibition/catalogue

Untitled form : reduction fired ceramic on marble base: 78cm high:
Made March 1991.
Maker: Jane Jones, The Studio, 35 East Street, Ludlow
(0876 543213)
Photo Credit: Peter Ogalvie

Updating slide libraries and indexes

When you have new photographs taken send these to slide indexes which contain slides of your work as it is important to continually update these. This is particularly important if you have done a new commission as future work may come from someone seeing the slide and wanting a similar piece of work. Have a look at your slides on indexes from time to time and remove any old ones which are now a cause of embarrassment!

Health & Safety

 Craft workshops are potentially hazardous places and as you will have no income if you are injured or fall ill, you must take care to try and cut down the risks.

Too often craftspeople work with unsafe machinery which endangers both themselves and others working in or visiting the workshop. Also craftspeople are sometimes ignorant of the dangers caused by exposure to dust, fumes and harmful materials. Illnesses related to these hazards can take years to manifest themselves, so always be on the look-out for advance warning signs, such as headaches, coughs, asthma, dizziness, etc. If you often feel under the weather when you are in the workshop but better away from it, then this is a strong indication that something at work is affecting you. This point cannot be emphasised too strongly. Sadly there are many instances of craftspeople having to give up their work as a result of continuous exposure to harmful materials.

Given the variety of hazards encountered in different crafts, it is not possible to do more than give some general guidance. For fuller information it is well worth obtaining a copy of "HEALTH & SAFETY" by Tim Challis and Gary Roberts, published by Artic Producers.

The workshop

Be aware of the fire escape routes from your workshop and ensure that these are kept unobstructed at all times. Keep a fire extinguisher in the workshop and check it regularly. Note that water extinguishers must not be used either on electrical fires, burning oils or solvents. Your local fire station will advise on types of fire extinguishers for your activities. Check that all wiring is safe and that everything is earthed.

Keep the workshop clean and tidy, and the floor clear of anything you might trip over or slip on. You should regularly vacuum or wet-mop to keep the dust down; dry brushing will only move the dust around.

It is best not to smoke in the workshop or to eat or drink there, as this can increase the chance of accidentally ingesting hazardous materials. If you work from home, do not contaminate your living area and never use the kitchen area as a work space. It is illegal to pour toxic chemicals down the drain, and inadvisable to pour any chemicals down the drain unless safely diluted.

Always have a source of fresh air in the workshop – an open window or air intake. For many activities, additional ventilation will be essential. If you create dust, then you should consider installing a purpose built extraction system. At the very least a vacuum cleaner set up next to the dust source can be helpful. All dust can be harmful and it is essential that you protect yourself from inhalation of dust as otherwise there may be a detrimental effect on your future health. For toxic materials you must always wear a face mask and use a strong exhaust fan to draw harmful materials and fumes away from your face. Use a spray booth for spraying glazes, paints, etc. All kilns and furnaces should be ventilated via a canopy hood or chimney to the outside. Make certain that any outlet is well away from air intakes.

You need to work in sufficient light, ideally natural light with artificial lighting merely supplementing it.

Protective clothing

Dust, flying fragments or splashes of harmful materials can damage your eyes so wear goggles where necessary. Dark green spectacles need to be worn if you are working with furnaces to protect your eyes from harmful infra-red rays. It may also be necessary to protect your hands and when handling materials, unless you know them to be completely safe wear rubber gloves. As your skin can become allergic to certain materials after prolonged handling it is easier to protect them to avoid this occurring. Stout footwear can reduce the danger of injury from falling weights or spilled liquids. Keep your clothing free of dust.

Equipment and materials

Adequate guarding of machinery is vital and certain equipment, especially wood and metal-working machinery, must be guarded by law – these guards should always be used. When you are using machinery, tie back long hair, restrain flapping clothing and remove any jewellery/rings which could catch in machinery. Leave adequate space around machinery and check it regularly. Badly designed equipment can cause back strain and it is worth investigating this when you are purchasing it.

Kilns should be located in a separate room from your general work area with the operating instructions clearly written nearby. If you do not have a separate space then at least try to create a separation between the work areas by a false wall or heavy plastic sheeting.

Be careful with materials, even those which are labelled non-toxic, for some materials labelled thus in the past have since been shown to have harmful effects. Again, watch out for tell-tale signs. Many illnesses caused by chemicals result from a long build-up of poisons in the body and certain chemicals can combine to produce even more dangerous effects. You therefore need to know the exact identity of all materials you are using and you should check for any toxicity. Glazes, dyes, chemicals, etc. can be potentially harmful and, given that dermatitis is common, it is essential that you take precautions. Wear rubber gloves where possible and wash hands and nails thoroughly after handling materials and after all work periods. Work surfaces should be kept clean and should be impervious – an untreated wooden surface will tend to retain harmful chemicals. Be especially careful if you have minor cuts and abrasions. If you use toxic materials, it is worth having your workshop regularly tested for contamination by the Health and Safety Inspector.

Keep a well-stocked first aid box handy in the workshop. If you are employing people you must record all injuries to employees in an "accident" book.

If you need any advice on specific points relating to health and safety at work, contact your local office of Health and Safety Executive. As well as offering advice and information, the Executive issues a number of useful booklets relating to specific industries and problems.

Staying healthy

Fixing some rules for hours/days worked is useful, for example, not more than ten hours in any one day (with occasional exceptions) and at least one day off every week. Stop for short rests over a cup of tea or coffee, have a decent break or short walk at lunch time, and stop when you feel over-tired.

Watch what you eat – it is easy to eat irregularly or badly when under pressure – and what you drink – hangovers will slow you down and, while no-one will breathalyse you while in charge of your business, alcohol can dissipate time and money and increase the chance of accidents in the workspace.

Be careful when lifting and carrying weights. If you are working in a fixed position for a time, take short breaks to ease the muscles. Similarly, if you are working for a long period on small, concentrated details give your eyes periodic rests.

Take holidays. Even a short break can help recharge your batteries and give you renewed energy and enthusiasm. If you find taking holidays hard, go off somewhere relaxing on a design research trip!

If you do get ill, do not struggle on and make yourself worse. Better to take one day off immediately than four days off later; if you are under the weather your efficiency may be so low that you might as well be in bed.

Coping with problems

Worrying about problems can make you ill. There are bound to be points of crisis so try and learn to cope with them as best you can. Worry, depression and fatigue create a state of mind where all problems take on the same weight, so the first thing to do is to try and put your problems in perspective. Several fairly minor problems can combine and seem overwhelming, so attempt to separate them out and assess each one in turn. Making a list might help. Then tackle each problem individually and in turn.

Do not let problems drag on. It is a common failing to ignore problems in the hope that they will go away, but for every one that does nine get worse! Tackling problems quickly will nearly always make them easier to sort out and stop them niggling away at the back of your mind.

Do not hesitate to seek help or advice from relevant organisations. If you are in doubt as to whom to turn to for help you can always approach the Crafts Council – even if they cannot help directly, they will at least point you in the right direction.

Forget your problems for a while by going for a walk, visiting an exhibition or having a short break. Often you will find this gives you fresh energy to tackle things.

Sources of Information and Advice

 The aim of this chapter is to provide a guide to the main national and regional funding bodies concerned with the crafts and to provide contact addresses of organisations who offer advice and information and other support for the crafts.

While there are a number of grants available as what is on offer tends to change from time to time only a few grant schemes are detailed You should research every possible source of financial support and check with relevant bodies to obtain information on their current schemes. To research possible schemes visit the Crafts Council Library or your local reference library and look through some of the guides to current grant and loan support for businesses to see if there are any which might be relevant. (see book list at the end of this chapter) You should also contact your local council - usually the Enterprise or Small Business Development Section - for relevant information

National funding bodies

CRAFTS COUNCIL
44A Pentonville Road
London, N1 9BY
0171 278 7700
e-mail: craft@craftscouncil.org.uk
web site: http:www.craftscouncil.org.uk
Open Tuesday-Saturday 11-6, Sunday 2-6, Closed Monday.
England and Wales

The Crafts Council is the national organisation for contemporary crafts in England and Wales and has its headquarters at the above address. The Council funds the ten English Regional Arts Boards and the Arts Council of Wales to support the crafts throughout England and Wales and also and provides a number of direct services. The Council receives a grant from the Scottish Arts Council for services for makers in Scotland. The London premises contain Britain's largest crafts gallery with a continuous programme of craft exhibitions, a shop selling craft objects and craft books, a cafe and an extensive Reference Section. The Crafts Council also has a national collection of contemporary craft works, publishes Crafts Magazine, runs Chelsea Crafts Fair, takes groups of British makers to trade fairs in Europe and America and manages a shop based at the Victoria and Albert Museum.

The Reference Section which is open to personal callers, contains books, current and back copies of relevant craft magazines and catalogues; business, marketing and export information and historical and critical material on the crafts. Other information available includes details on full-time, part-time and short courses in the crafts, forthcoming craft fairs, craft shops and galleries, guilds and societies, craft materials and equipment, group workshops and postcard printers.

There is an electronic Photostore which holds over 35,000 images of work by selected makers, items from the Council's collection, exhibitions and the work of recent Setting Up and SAC Start Up Grant recipients. Images can be viewed at the London offices and prints can be purchased. Slides of the work are avilable on loan, either direct from the Council or by post at a nominal charge. The Centre also houses the Index of Selected Makers (around 600 makers) and the National Register of Makers. The Crafts Council Register consists of a card index of makers, divided according to craft and county, and is open to all professional craftsmen and women working in England, Scotland and Wales. Everyone who is registered receives a free copy of the bi-annual publication "Makers News". The Council receives many enquiries about craftspeople who undertake commissions, take part in exhibitions, give talks, etc. so it is worthwhile ensuring that you are included. Details on the Register and how to apply for the Selected Index are available from the Reference Section.

The Crafts Council can also help with specific problems encountered in running a business or marketing work, and you should not hesitate to get in touch in writing if you need help or advice.

SETTING UP SCHEME: grant scheme to assist selected craftspeople in England and Wales set up a first workshop (contact Scottish Arts Council for details of their equivalent scheme if based in Scotland). Maintenance grant of £2,500 for one year and 50% of the cost of purchasing or hiring essential equipment up to maximum of £5,000 (50% of £10,000). Must be within two years of setting up. Contact the Information Centre at the CC asking for the information pack 'Setting Up in Business' which includes an application form.

THE ARTS COUNCIL OF ENGLAND
14 Great Peter Street
London, SW1P 3NQ
0171 333 0100
The Arts Council has responsibility for painting, fine scuplture and photography.

Regional Arts Boards / Arts Council of Wales / Scottish Arts Council

The ten Regional Arts Boards in England, the Scottish Arts Council and Arts Council of Wales all have specialist art and craft departments. The assistance available is different in each organisation but the types of services on offer can include specialised training courses for craftspeople, slide indexesin which you may be able to have your slides included and newsletters for craftspeople. Some offer grants or loans, for example, to print promotional literature, research and develop new ideas or undertake special projects, buy equipment, to attend craft or trade fairs, prepare work for exhibition and travel abroad. All are good sources of information and advice and contact can lead to your work being promoted or your skills being used in residencies or school placements, for public commissions, the stocking of craft shops and so on. Contact the one relevant to the area in which you work.

LONDON ARTS BOARD
Elme House
133 Long Acre
London, WC2E 9AF
0171 240 1313
32 London boroughs and the Corporation of the City of London

NORTHERN ARTS
9-10 Osbourne Terrace
Jesmond
Newcastle upon Tyne, NE2 1NZ
0191 281 6334
Cumbria, Durham, Northumberland; unitary authorities of Darlington, Hartlepool, Middlesbrough, Redcar and Cleveland, Stockton; metropolitan districts of Newcastle, Gateshead, North Tyneside, Sunderland and South Tyneside.

EASTERN ARTS BOARD
Cherry Hinton Hall
Cherry Hinton Road
Cambridge, CB1 4DW
01223 215355
Bedfordshire, Cambridgeshire, Essex, Hertfordshire, Norfolk, Suffolk; unitary authority of Luton

NORTH WEST ARTS BOARD
Manchester House
22 Bridge Street
Manchester, M3 3AB
0161 834 6644
Cheshire, Lancashire, Merseyside, Greater Manchester and High Peak District of Derbyshire

East Midlands Arts Board
Mountfields House
Epinal Way
Loughborough, LE11 0QE
01509 218292
Derbyshire (excluding High Peak District), Leicestershire, Northamptonshire, Nottinghamshire; unitary authorities of Derby, Leicester and Rutland.

South East Arts Board
10 Mount Ephraim
Tunbridge Wells
Kent, TN4 8AS
01892 515210
Kent, Surrey, East Sussex, West Sussex; unitary authority of Brighton and Hove.

South West Arts
Bradninch Place
Gandy Street
Exeter, EX4 3LS
01392 218188
Cornwall, Devon, Dorset (except districts of Bournemouth, Christchurch and Poole), Gloucestershire and Somerset; unitary authorities of Bristol, Bath and North East Somerset, South Gloucestershire, North Somerset.

Yorkshire & Humberside Arts
21 Bond Street
Dewsbury, WF13 1AX
01924 455555
North Yorkshire; unitary authorities of York, Hull, East Riding, North Lincolnshire, North East Lincolnshire; metropolitan districts of Barnsley, Bradford, Calderdale, Doncaster, Kirklees, Leeds, Rotherham, Sheffield, Wakefield.

Southern Arts Board
13 St Clement Street
Winchester, S023 9DQ
01962 855099
Berkshire, Hampshire, Isle of Wight, Oxfordshire, Wiltshire, south east Dorset; unitary authorities of Bournmouth, Milton Keynes, Poole, Portsmouth, Southampton, Swindon

Arts Council of Wales
Holst House
9 Museum Place
Cardiff, CF1 3NX
Wales.
01222 394711
Wales only

West Midlands Arts Board
82 Granville Street
Birmingham, B1 2LH
0121 631 3121
Hereford & Worcester, Shropshire, Staffordshire, Warwickshire; metropolitan districts of Birmingham, Coventry, Dudley, Sandwell, Solihull, Walsall and Wolverhampton; unitary authority of Stoke-on Trent.

Scottish Arts Council
12 Manor Place
Edinburgh, EH3 7DD
0131 226 6051
Scotland only

Other regional funding bodies

Wales

WELSH DEVELOPMENT AGENCY
Head Office:
Principality House
The Friary
Cardiff, CF1 4AE
0345 775566
All Wales. Main agency for promotion of Welsh economy. Support includes business advice, venture capital schemes, conversion grants and loan schemes.

THE DEVELOPMENT BOARD FOR RURAL WALES
Ladywell House
Park Street
Newtown
Powys, SY16 1JB
01686 626965

Scotland

MADE IN SCOTLAND
The Craft Centre
Station Road
Beauly
Inverness-shire, IV4 7EH
01463 782578
All Scotland. Provides a range of marketing advice and assistance to craft businesses. It also organises and promotes trade fairs and produces promotional material for the industry.

HIGHLAND AND ISLAND ENTERPRISE
Bridge House
20 Bridge Street
Inverness, IV1 1QR
01463 234171
Gives advice to business in setting up, developing and expanding in the N&W part of Scotland (Shetland, Orkney, The Western Isles, Highland Region, W Moray district, Isle of Arran, The Cumbraes and Argyll and Bute district). Will refer individuals to local LECs for financial support.

Scottish Enterprise
120 Bothwell Street
Glasgow, G2 7JP
0141 248 2700
Similar role to H & I Enterprise, covering Ayrshire, Scottish borders, Dumfries & Galloway, Dumbartonshire, Fife and Forth Valley, Teeside, Renfrewshire, Lothian, Lanarkshire and Grampian.

Northern Ireland

Local Enterprise Development Unit (LEDU)
LEDU House
Upper Galwally
Belfast, BT8 4TB
01232 491031
Northern Ireland only. Small business agency, focusing on businesses with less than 50 employees, providing a folio of assistance including development, marketing, technical and where appropriate financial support.

Other bodies who provide assistance with setting up or expanding a business

LIVEWIRE
Head Office:
Livewire
Freepost
Newcastle upon Tyne, NE1 1BR
0191 261 5584
(Contact above address for regional offices).
Assists 16-30 year olds in England, Scotland and Wales to set up and expand their businesses by putting them in touch with a business advisor who will help them put together a business plan. Also offer cash awards through Start Up Awards and Business Growth Challenge Scheme. Sponsored by Shell UK Ltd. Contact head office for details of local offices.

TRAINING ENTERPRISE COUNCILS (TECS) in England and Wales and LOCAL ENTERPRISE COMPANIES (LECS) in Scotland.
The TECs and LECs manage and develop Government sponsored initiatives such as Youth Training, Employment Training, Business and Enterprise Training and Business Start Up Scheme. Payments for the Business Start Up Scheme (BSUS) are between £20 and £90 a week, length of support can be from 26 to 66 weeks. Before going on the scheme applicants will be given training in business skills leading to the production of a Business Plan. Applicants should normally have been in receipt of Job Seekers Allowance for 6 weeks at the time of applying and should be able to invest £1,000 in the business, however there are some exceptions to this ruling. Addresses of local TECs/LECs available through Job centres or ring freephone number 0345 100412 (OUTSIDE LONDON) or 0171 735 0010 (LONDON)

LOCAL ENTERPRISE AGENCIES

There are more than 300 LEAs in England funded by a partnership of local and national companies, local authorities, TECs and central government. They provide business information and advice, help in preparing a business plan and assistance in identifying other sources of help for small businesses. Some LEAs charge for their services. Ask your local Jobcentre for details.

RURAL DEVELOPMENT COMMISSION

Head Offices:
19 Dacre Street
London, SW1H ODH
0171 276 6969
or
141 Castle Street
Salisbury
Wilts, SP1 3TP
01722 336255
(Contact above address for regional offices).

Main aim is to stimulate job creation and provision of essential services in the countryside. Support only available in rural areas and country towns with a population of up 10,000 and to businesses with less than 20 employees. Priority given to those in Rural Development Areas and in other priority areas which have been designated in 30 English countries.

REDUNDANT BUILDINGS GRANT SCHEME

Grants of up to 25% of the costs of conversion of redundant buildings in Priority Areas and in some other designated areas. The RDC also offers workshop units for sale or rent through English Estates.

Governments schemes

There are a number of Government Schemes which focus on assisting new businesses starting up within designated priority areas ("Assisted Areas"). These include Development, City Challenge, Scottish Urban and Enterprise Zone Areas. The Department of Trade and Industry (DTI) may be able to help businesses in Assisted Areas by offering REGIONAL ENTERPRISE GRANTS for innovation (in its Development and Intermediate Areas) and investment projects (in Development Areas). REGIONAL SELECTIVE ASSISTANCE is available (in both Development and Intermediate Areas) for projects that create or safeguard employment and clearly show that they bring regional or national benefit with them. Contact the DTI on 0171 215 2564 for details of geographical areas covered and for addresses of regional offices.

LOCAL CHAMBERS OF COMMERCE or small business units of LOCAL COUNCILS AND TOURIST OFFICES can also be worth approaching if you have a query relevant to them.

Charitable trusts

There are a number of charitable trusts and foundations which offer annual bursaries and awards for specific projects which can include a craft category. This list gives some of the major ones but there are smaller trusts such as the Theo Moorman Charitable Trust, Edward Marshall Trust, David Canter Memorial Fund and the Wingate Scholarships which often provide support for craftspeople. Information on these and others can be obtained by regularly scanning the opportunities/awards sections of publications such as Crafts, Artists Newsletter, Regional Arts Board newsletters or consulting the Directory of Grant Making Trusts.

The Princes Youth Business Trust (PYBT)
Head Office:
18 Park Square East
London, NW1Y 4LH
0171 543 1234
(Contact above address for regional offices).
Charity which helps young people in the 18-29 age group (up to 30 for disabled people) set up or develop their own businesses in England, Scotland and Wales. Need to have been unemployed for at least six weeks (unless under notice for redundancy), have a viable business plan, be unable to raise the funds from other sources and demonstrate being from a "less fortunate background".
Financial support available through
Bursaries (grants) of up to £1500 to individuals or of £3000 to groups of young people to start a business. For purchasing equipment, transport, fees, insurance and training.
Low interest Loans of up to £5000 for stock, equipment or working capital.
Test Marketing Grants of up to £250 to test the market when there is not enough proof of a need for the goods or service they are thinking of providing.
European Marketing Grants of up to £350 to attend a continental Trade Fair or specialist exhibition or to develop links with European partners.
The Trust also allocates a volunteer business adviser to everyone who receives money from the PYBT, takes groups to trade fairs and organises its own annual trade show.

THE PRINCE'S TRUST - ACTION
18 Park Square East
London
NW1 4LH
[Note: not to be confused with the PYBT - the Prince's Trust is a separate organisation.]
The European Programme aims to help young people aged 18 - 25, no longer in full-time education and finding life tough. It provides help with travel and living costs to enable young people to do voluntary work in Europe or to explore an idea for a project with a European counterpart.

THE FOUNDATION FOR SPORT AND THE ARTS
Grattan Endicott, Secretary to the Trustees
The Foundation for Sport and the Arts
PO Box 20
Liverpool, L13 1HB
0151 259 5505
The Foundation is an independent trust privately funded from the football pools and seeks to encourage and fund the Sport and the Arts by enhancing the quality of life for the community generally. Individuals seeking funding should contact the Foundation on the above number.

THE ARTS LOTTERY
There are separate Arts Lottery bodies in England, Scotland and Wales funded by proceeds from the National Lottery. Lottery funds are available for capital projects in the crafts and this could include the purchase or refurbishment of premises to be used as a group workshop or exhibition gallery, and the purchase of a pool of equipment by a group of craftspeople.
Contact the appropriate Arts Council for details.

THE WINSTON CHURCHILL MEMORIAL TRUST
15 Queen's Gate Terrace
London, SW7 5PR
0171- 584 9315
About 11 awards made annually to UK citizens to enable individuals to gain a better understanding of the lives and work of people in overseas countries. Specific catagories given each year.

Other useful contacts

BRITISH COUNCIL
Visual Arts Department
11 Portland Place
London W1N 4EJ
0171 930 8466

Britain's main agent for cultural relations overseas. Seeks to promote an understanding and appreciation of cultural, educational matters and technical co-operation between Britain and other countries. The Visual Arts Department is concerned with the promotion and presentation abroad of British Art and Craft.

The GRANTS TO ARTISTS EXHIBITING ABROAD scheme is designed to help assist professional British artists and craftspeople resident in the UK to exhibit overseas in public or commercial spaces. Awards are also given in connection with workshop projects which are professionally organised and which involve the participation of artists from the host country.

Design Council
Haymarket House
1 Oxenden Street
London, SW1Y 4EE
0171 208 2121
The Design Council aims to inspire the best use of design by the UK, in a world context in order to improve prosperity and well being. It works with business, education and the public sector, to increase awareness and use of design.

Federation of Small Businesses
140 Lower Marsh
Westminster Bridge
London, SE1 7AE
0171 928 9272
Membership organisation, funded by its members. Operates mainly as a pressure group on behalf of small businesses who are members (costs from £80 a year), covering taxation, planning, with 24 hour legal advice line and advice on insurance.

Guilds & associations

There are a range of craft guilds, both national and regional, and all promote contact between craftspeople. All will help with information and a number assist in promoting and selling members' work. Before deciding to join any crafts body, check to see that it is relevant and of use. A list of all guilds is available from the Crafts Council's Information Section.

Craft commissioning agencies

Listed below are some of the main agencies which operate to develop commissions for craftspeople and artists in public spaces or buildings. In addition to these agencies most Regional Arts Boards work directly on the development of craft commissions (for example South West Arts employs a commissioning officer) and it is worth contacting your regional board to find about their approach to commissioning.

If you are interested in working to commission you can contact these agencies to see if your work would be of interest. Many have slide indexes which you may be able to join.

ART IN PARTNERSHIP - SCOTLAND
233 Cowgate
Edinburgh EH1 1JQ
0131 225 4463

ARTPOINT
North Paviliion
Parklands
Great Linford
Milton Keynes MK14 5DZ
01908 606791

ARTISTS AGENCY
1st & 2nd Floors
18 Norfolk Street
Sunderland SR1 1EA
0191 510 9318

COMMISSIONS EAST
St Giles Hall
Pound Hill
Cambridge CB3 0AE
01223 356882

ARTWORKS WALES
2 John Street
Cardiff CF1 5AE
01222 489543

CONTEMPORARY APPLIED ARTS
2 Percy Street
London W1P 9FA
tel: 0171 436 2344
fax: 0171 436 2446

ORIEL CRAFT & DESIGN SERVICE
Oriel
The Friary
Cardiff CF1 4AA
01222 395548

PARTNERSHIP ART LTD
Providence Mill
Alexandra Street
Hyde
Cheshire SK14 1DX
0161 367 8640

PUBLIC ART COMMISSIONS AGENCY
Studio 6
Victoria Works
Vittoria Street
Birmingham B1 3PE
0121 212 4454

PUBLIC ART DEVELOPMENT TRUST
3rd Floor, Kirkman House
12-14 Whitfield Street
London W1P 5RD
0171 580 9977
Fax: 0171 580 8540

PUBLIC ARTS
24 Bond Street
Wakefield WF1 2QP
01924 295791

MEMORIALS BY ARTISTS
Snape Priory
Saxmundham
Suffolk IP17 1SA
01728 68 8934
Specialises in the commissioning of memorials.

Reference books

These publications are available for reference in the Crafts Council Reference Section (along with the other books mentioned on this list) or ask at your own central reference library.

General Funding/Charitable Trust Funding Guides

These provide information on grants, loans and assistance for small businesses.

NEW SOURCES OF GRANTS AND AID FOR BUSINESSES IN THE UK
Published by WEKA Publishing

A-Z OF BUSINESS INFORMATION SOURCES, published by Croners, 1993

THE ARTS FUNDING GUIDE 1994, Edited by Anne Marie Doulton, published by Directory of Social Change

THE GRANTS REGISTER, 1993-95, Edited by Lisa Williams, published by Macmillan

THE DIRECTORY OF GRANT MAKING TRUSTS, 13th Edition 1993-94, published by Charities Aid Foundation

HANDBOOK OF GRANTS, Edited by Maggie Heath & Graeme Farnell, published by The Museum Development Company

SOURCES OF GRANTS AND AID FOR BUSINESSES, Volumes 1 & 2 (a practical guide to the financial support and advisory services available to UK businesses from central government, local authorities and regional agencies), Edited by Anthony Harrison, published by GEE

The Hollis Arts Funding Handbook, 1996/97 (third edition)
Edited by Angus Broadbent. Includes national, regional and international sections, published by Hollis Directories.

Charities Digest
Edited and published by The Family Welfare Association.

How to apply for Grant, loans and other sources of finance
by Harris Rosenberg, published by GEE

Business Information Books

A range of books of particular relevance to the crafts are listed, but there are many others which might be useful. The Croners reference books mentioned are directed at all small businesses and updated monthly so information is current. These are particularly helpful on legal points.

Reference Book for the Self-Employed and Smaller Businesses
Published by Croners

Health and Safety at work
Published by Croners

Europe, Vol 1 & 2
Published by Croners

European Business Information Sources
Published by Croners

Model commercial contracts and letters
published by GEE

Crafts and visual arts information books

This list is by no means exhaustive. A range of books of particular relevance to the crafts are listed, but there are many others which might be useful.

MONEY MATTERS: THE ARTISTS FINANCIAL GUIDE
By Sarah Deeks, Richard Murphy & Sally Nolan Price, AN Publications.

FUNDRAISING: THE ARTIST'S GUIDE TO PLANNING AND FINANCING WORK
Ed Susan Jones, AN Publications

SELLING
By Judith Staines
AN Publications.

MAKING CONNECTIONS: THE CRAFTSPERSON'S GUIDE TO EUROPE
By Judith Staines, South West Arts

ACROSS EUROPE: THE ARTIST'S PERSONAL GUIDE TO TRAVEL AND WORK
Ed David Butler, AN Publications

EXHIBITING AND SELLING ABROAD
By Judith Staines, AN Publications

ORGANISING YOUR EXHIBITION: THE SELF-HELP GUIDE
By Debbie Duffin, AN Publications

DIRECTORY OF EXHIBITION SPACES
Ed Richard Padwick, AN Publications

PUBLIC ART - PEOPLE, PROJECTS, PROCESS
Southern Band and Eileen Adams

ART WITHIN REACH - ARTISTS & CRAFTWORKERS, ARCHITECTS & PATRONS IN THE MAKING OF PUBLIC ART
edited Peter Townsend pub. by Art Monthly/Arts Council of Great Britain/Crafts Council

THE FURNISHED LANDSCAPE - APPLIED ART IN PUBLIC PLACES
by Patrick Nuttgens, Floris Van Den Broecke, Jane Heath & John Houston
pub. by Bellew Publishing, Crafts Council and the Arts Council

AN PUBLICATIONS also produce a SERIES OF FACTPACKS on, for example, Slide Indexes, Visual Arts Contracts, Rates of Pay, Mailing the Press, Craft Fairs, Insurance, Buying Clay, Buying a Kiln, New Technology. Prices £1.85 - £3.50.

Books and factpacks are available from the Crafts Council Bookshop, Islington and by mail order from AN Publications, PO Box 23, Sunderland SR4 3DG.
Tel 0191-514 3600

Specialist magazines

There are a number of specialist craft magazines such as Ceramic Review and Studio Pottery. The two magazines most relevant to all makers are *Crafts* and *Artist's Newsletter.*

CRAFTS is bi-monthly, published by the Crafts Council, and contains news, features on contemporary crafts, details of shops and galleries, forthcoming exhibitions, information on competitions, residencies, etc., and a useful advertisement section.

ARTIST'S NEWSLETTER is published monthly by AN Publications,
PO Box 23,
Sunderland SR4 63DG.
Tel 0191-514 3600
An extremely useful magazine, concentrating on information for artists and craftspeople. It includes details of residencies, open exhibitions, competitions and awards, plus features on specific subjects such as publicity, marketing, commissioning and craft fairs.

Notes

Notes

Notes